Wait on the Lord

How to Connect Your Soul to the Lord by Waiting on Him

Wait on the Lord

How to Connect Your Soul to the Lord by Waiting on Him

Lami Abayilo

Take note that the name satan and related names are not capitalized. We choose not to acknowledge him, even to the point of violating grammatical rules.

DESTINY IMAGE EUROPE
Via Maiella, 1
66020 San Giovanni Teatino (Ch) - Italy

ISBN: 88-89127-08-2

1 2 3 4 5 6 7 8/10 09 08 07 06 05

This book and all other Destiny Image Europe books are available at Christian bookstores and distributors worldwide.

To order products, or for any other correspondence:

DESTINY IMAGE EUROPE
Via Acquacorrente, 6
65123 - Pescara - Italy
Tel. +39 085 4716623 - Fax: +39 085 4716622
E-mail: info@eurodestinyimage.com

Or reach us on the Internet:

www.eurodestinyimage.com

Contents

Foreword

This book dares you to "experience God." As you ride along with the author of these precious nuggets of reality, you will be convinced of the essence of waiting on the Lord. These inspiring, life-changing and soul-building experiences will show you how to rely on, depend upon and ultimately wait upon the Lord Jesus Christ, who is the only way, the reality and the life.

In this storehouse full of soul food and unseen realities, you will see the reasons and benefits of why you desperately need to wait on the Lord.

Remember that *"he who comes to God must believe that He is and that He is a rewarder of those who diligently seek him"* (Hebrew 11:6).

The author recounts real-life encounters as she waited significantly in His presence, and experienced the ability of mounting up with wings like eagles, running but not growing weary, walking and not fainting, and thereby fulfilling the very fact that Scripture can never be broken.

Finally, as you behold the beauty of the Lord in this book, may you find the Holy Spirit, who is the angel of "His presence," to be ever present in the times of your life.

Franklyn Abayilo

INTRODUCTION

Wholeness in His Presence

It is such a delight to share these nuggets of truth from the presence of the Lord. This book stems from a personal relationship with Him, and the truths contained within have come to rest in my spirit along the course of life's journey. Until I met Jesus Christ in a personal and intimate way, my life was a constant mess of failure, pain, confusion and broken relationships. Moving beyond that, I have come to walk in the revelation knowledge of eternal life, which He gives without shadow of turning. Not only did I get a grasp of His eternal love, but I also discovered what it means to sincerely wait on Him, and gather the momentum needed for all levels of my walk with Him. As I entrusted my life to Him and made a conscious decision to continually wait on Him, my life has been transformed to "wholeness." I have come to realize waiting on the Lord as a way-of-life for those of us who are joints heirs with Him. As such, this manner of existence becomes a daily revelation.

We live in a world full of limitations, resistance and challenges. Therefore, we need to understand God's perspective for living. We often find ourselves asking the question, “How can we live a sane life in this world full of pressures?” At every opportunity, we want to jump in and fix things ourselves. But we are not called to be “fixers” who run ahead of the Shepherd of our soul. We are called wait in His presence. Without Him, our souls will always be dry, thirsty and in longing because an absence of His presence creates a deep void. This emptiness will constantly expand without the infilling of His presence. So, in an attempt to fill-up this emptiness, we go from one experience to another, trying to lay hold of anything within our grasp. Having done everything we can think of to satisfy our innermost cravings and desires, we end up no happier than when we first began the journey.

Many people in today’s world go through life never really comprehending the beauty of being whole in spirit, soul and body. I had gone through life to some extent broken, dissatisfied and distressed. I never knew what I wanted out of life or if it had any purpose for me. It took me more than going before God at the altar and saying the Sinner’s Prayer to get to the point where I could say boldly and with confidence, *“The joy of the Lord is my strength.”* God’s heart desire for all of us is to come to the saving knowledge of Jesus Christ: that is the very reason why He gave up His life for us.

But it is necessary to walk in a depth of God’s presence, if our lives are to have a true, deep and lasting meaning, as well as peace amidst all the surrounding chaos. Such depth is a joyous realm of ecstasy that comes from constantly waiting on Him. Without the revelation of eternal life in our spirit, we will be stuck in a world of discontentment that sinks our soul into a cyclical abyss of purposelessness and hopelessness. My heart’s desire is that you will step into that “waiting mode” and go with Him one step at a time. While doing so, you will suddenly realize that you have been made whole. Your life will become put together with a rich anointing all over it. You will no longer be fragmented because the Author of life has breathed "eternal life" into your spirit.

This will enable you to live victoriously on this side of Heaven. You will experience an intimate relationship with the One who holds all power in His mighty hands. By waiting in His presence, you will discover well-springs of intimacy and peace that surpasses all human understanding. As you journey through these pages, my sincere prayer is for you to acquire a highest degree of a daily hunger and thirst for His presence in your life. As you hunger and thirst after Him, you shall be filled. May you also fully comprehend that waiting on the Lord has absolutely nothing to do with a set of regimented rules-and-regulations, but rather a step-by-step ushering-in into His presence.

"Afterward Jesus findeth him in the temple, and said unto him, Behold thou are made whole: sin no more, least a worse thing come unto thee" (John 5:14 KJV). Just like Jesus found this man in the temple—which is the meeting place where humanity and holiness blend together—may He find you so as to make you whole and give you "the reason for life" which is Christ in you the hope of glory. Life in Christ is so very real. Understanding the efficacy of this life is very important because after all is said and done, what truly matters is the quality of how you lived. Yes, you may have struggles and issues to be dealt with, as we all do. But, know that beyond your issues lies the love of God. That love is so tangible that it reaches out to the darkest hours of humanity and brings restoration where all hope is lost.

He wants us to walk in the revelation and reality of the "new creation man." The man with eternal life rooted in his spirit stays on top when all else is caving in. Who you are, where you have been and what you have done does not matter. What does matter is that you make a connection with His presence and then watch as you transform into what He wants you to be. When this occurs, you can maximize abundant life above everything that had once hindered you.

I became so enamored with His presence to the point that it became easy to reckon with the dead past: I dealt with issues that needed dealing with and moved onto a greater and higher walk in Him. I know many people who have come to Christ still struggle with issues and don't know how to appropriate the victory that Jesus Christ wrought at Calvary. Many sermons have been preached and books written on the subject of *"Wait on the Lord."*

But my objective is for you to understand that even with a life full of struggles from the pressures of the flesh and besetting sins, you can have complete restoration and wholeness in His presence. You may be hanging-on with a lot of mess and confusion and not know what to do. But know that by cleaving onto His presence, the restorer is on His way to your heart. Your life will gain its worth and deep intrinsic values when you make that connection with His presence. Resurrection power will come upon you so mightily that you will take charge of situations around you and live in the supernatural, all because you dared to wait on the Lord.

CHAPTER 1

Swapping Plans

If the Lord is not the center of your life, then you will be presented with overwhelming complexities. In most cases, life itself is like an instructor: it will give you lessons geared towards where your heart is channeled. Depending on whose side you are on, life will teach you according to plans made either within or outside God's anointing. If your life is channeled toward the course of eternity, certainly your experiences will not be overbearing and purposeless because the user's manual—the Word of God—will teach and guide you through it. On the other hand, if you go about making your plans without Him, you will someday have to face the music you played for yourself.

This is the reason why what happens to you outside His presence is a threat to your peace. You may have made great plans and thought you knew the direction for your life. You brought a self-designed map and embarked on the journey without the Master Planner. Then suddenly, your world took a different turn and started to crash-in on you. You cannot believe everything that is happening to you. Why don't you have the joy, peace, laughter and serenity that you thought would be yours when your plans took their course? You are in a mess and desperately need a way out. As far as the straight path of life is concerned, yours has been very inconsistent: it is always to jump in and out of whatever the flesh demands. You wish it wasn't that way, but you can't help doing those things that keep you in bondage. Overpowering pressures are almost choking the confident peace out of you. You insist on a way out, but still can't find an exit, even after having tried so many things.

So you paused to take a look at your life. According to your own plans, you knew when you were supposed to graduate from college, get married, climb the success ladder and have a respectable life with all its niceties in place. You may have even attained all that success, and then moved to another level where you had all the glitter of the "good life." But the friends, money and partying left you feeling empty, broken and incomplete, despite all you acquired. You have it all, but you are dissatisfied and unfulfilled. Maybe you even believe that you are walking with God and, therefore, nothing can come close to messing up your plans.

Yes, you are supposed to have a relationship with the Master Planner, but your life is still missing something. You thought that by coming to Him, all would be made well. But alas, your life's boat is rocking on many storms threatening to sink the vessel. Have you become so exasperated that you are about to give up and throw in the towel? Right now, the Spirit of the Lord is saying, *"Come to me, all you who labor and are heavy laden, and I will give you rest."*[1] Finding rest for your soul will come as you wait on the Lord, which means dwelling in His presence, rendering service to Him, worshipping Him in spirit and truth, holding on to Him with an unchanging heart, and trusting Him despite contrary evidence. We have the assurance that the thoughts He has for us are good and not evil.[2] Therefore, we do not need to fear what the future holds. He knows the end picture from the beginning, and that is why we trust must completely wrap up our trust in Him because that will be "victory in your final outcome."

Right now you may be stuck somewhere between discontentment and confusion, even though in the Master's plan for your life, you should be walking in His rest for your soul. With all the loneliness, pain and frustrating challenges going on in your external and internal world, you need to pull aside and pursue God with all your might. Resolve to hear Him speak to you in the peace and quietness of your spirit. "God is Spirit and those who worship Him must worship Him in spirit and in truth."[3] He can only minister to your spirit. If your spirit is not in right fellowship with Him, you will waste time looking for wholeness in the wrong places. Whereas the answers to your life's questions are awaiting you in His presence.

As you begin to get into the attitude of waiting in God's presence, changes will start happening in your life as plans swap places. Your plans will pale in comparison to His plans. Everything you held on to so dearly begins to fade out. What you did when under control of the law of sin-and-death will become shadows in the light of He who is the life-giving Spirit. "Swapping plans" is all about restoration. You will see God take control of your life and restore wholeness to you from areas where the devil had you messed up and in deception. But you have to lay down everything before the altar of sacrifice. When you let go and let God, He will take preeminence in your life, and your plans will change into His glorious plans.

A solid foundation will be built inside you: works-of-the-flesh will give way as you begin to manifest fruit of the recreated spirit. He will work out a far exceeding weight of glory in you. He will mold and shape you into what He wants you to be. After all is said and done, your life will bring glory to His name. You are the clay in the potter's hands to be molded and fitted for the Master's display so that his multifaceted wisdom will be made known to nations of the earth through you.

The process of change for all who come to Him may be different, but the purpose remains the same: that Christ may dwell in you richly. He wants to present you complete in Him, so that you can win souls and affect lives for the Kingdom. What He does as you wait on Him is take you aside to pull down your walls of containment. He strips you from depending on people and things around you and makes it so that your eyes are completely fixed on Him. Only then will you get to know that He alone is the only true God, and that no other god exists besides Him. Only He can satisfy your soul's longing and fill the vacuum in your heart.

When everything else becomes shadow in the light of Him—and when your heart is fully lifted to Him in humility and you are calm in your spirit—that is when He shows up in a mighty and awesome way. In quietness and stillness, you will see Him ministering to create a sense of worth and value in you. He will take you up to different levels in life. He will reveal different levels of relationship with Him and with mankind. Your life will now have its created purpose because you know your God-given destination. You will ultimately know that you are not alone because His divine presence will be evident wherever you go. Even when the storms of life come against you—in pressure from situations you had not planned for—He is there to hold your hand through and, at other times, away from the storms.

Waiting on the Lord is a lifetime walk and understanding of spiritual matters. We cannot do without Him. He is our anchor and tower of strength. He is our direction. Left to us alone, we will drive our lives to destruction from an inability to make right choices rooted in His will. He is the answer to all of life's challenges and endeavors. He alone knows what life is all about. That is why you can never find the answers to life's questions in power, drugs, alcohol, sex and many other weights and works of the flesh. When you take that step of faith into His presence, you will see His grace made perfect in your weakness because… *"Those who wait on the Lord shall renew their strength"* (Isaiah 40:31).

In the Beginning

Therefore, if anyone is in Christ, he is a new creation; old things have passed away; behold all things have become new.[4]

The new creation man is that man who has no past. He never existed before. Born with the God-kind of life, everything about the spirit of the new creation man is brand new. You say, "Bravo that is I." But what do you do when you keep falling right back into that place of depravity, bitterness and rage, lack and hopelessness, and jealousy and anger. What do you do when your self-control fails every time? You do not want to do those things that eat away at your peace, yet you end up right back at that lack self-control. What do you do your plans do not have His signature endorsed on them? How did you get so hooked on the flesh? You are a new creation in Christ Jesus, but you struggle so much with the flesh. You are confused by the lifestyle of the sin nature that springs up on you. What do you do?

Many people are struggling with the sin nature. They say to themselves, "I have asked Him into my life, how come I still do these things? How come I don't have peace, joy and laughter?" So many nagging questions are left on your mind without answers. Until you get to that point of walking in the reality of the new life you have in Christ Jesus, you will continue to walk in defeat. As long as you have His nature within, you are operating in life with a higher power. But you must be conscious of that and develop a rich relationship with Him. Do you know what you have down in your spirit? Do you realize that the King of Kings and the Lord of Lords has given you life?

One night at about two minutes past midnight, I found myself still awake. Once again, I replayed scenes of my life as they came to my subconscious; I ought to have reckoned these scenes dead, in His presence. When I left work earlier that day, I really didn't want to go home to those silent inner screams, which had been the norm for a long time. I had a lot of distressing questions on my mind. I would have to be alone for a while before anyone else returned. I knew I had my leadership training at church, but going for training was the last thing I wanted to do. "What did I need some more training for?" I had nothing inside to give out. That was how empty I felt. It seemed as if all the joints of my life's different parts had come out of their sockets.

After so many struggles on the inside, I managed to get myself to church. Going to the house of the Lord should be a shared delight, but the weights we carry have a way of pulling us down. For the first time in my life, I blanked out in church. I am not sure I heard much of what the pastor said because pain and distress clustered my mind. In trying to understand my feelings, I found that I had many unresolved conflicts over issues buried deep within me. Sitting right there on my seat, this thought hit the core of my existence: real peace comes only in the presence of God.

I wondered about the many other people sitting down at the leadership training who had pressures bottled up inside. They are holding on to overwhelming pressures that have not been completely taken to the Lord. Instantly, I realized that so many people are doing things that count towards eternity, but a well-spring of unfulfillment remains buried deep within. The core of their foundation has pressures tucked away inside, and they carry lots of guilt and condemnation from the past. Scared to confront their issues, they do not know what to do.

In cross-examining myself, I realized that I was not walking in God's rest. "Why is that?" Then it dawned on me that I was walking after the flesh and not the Spirit. My internal pressure was a major distraction and, by now, I was walking with much guilt and condemnation. I lacked the boldness to take a plunge into the presence of the Most High. I knew about the peace of God that surpasses human understanding, but I lacked this peace. Walking and living such peace seemed far-fetched because I had not allowed Him to completely take over my issues. I kept thinking I could fix it all before going to Him. If I longed for anything at that moment, it was that peace which God gives without shadow of turning.

Strange Addictions

Although I had struggled with varying degrees of addictions, these were only symptoms of deeper, unresolved issues. The intense need to love and be loved led me to wrong relationships. Seeking to satisfy my desperate need to be touched, I medicated my pain with co-dependent relationships. In reading this now, you may be wondering what to do because you are hooked up on all sorts addictions. For the very reason that Jesus has made you complete in Him, you don't need anything else to give you fulfillment in life.

I kept struggling with these addictions because somewhere in the back of my mind, I had convinced myself that I could get right by myself. Little did I realize, that all I needed to do was walk in the revelation of the righteous nature I have in Him. Do you know that you can't save yourself? He alone can put your life together and give it meaning. You must give up everything at the altar of sacrifice to the One who is able to deliver you from your "strange addictions." Otherwise, you will struggle yourself to destruction. When you say "yes" to God, you are saying "yes" to righteousness. Therefore, you never have to work at being righteous:

when you identified with Him, you take on His very nature of righteousness.

As I matured in the things of God, I got to understand full well about the recreated human spirit. You see, man is a triune being: he is a spirit; he has a soul; and he lives in a body. It is the spirit that actually gets recreated and not the mind. You will have to feed your mind with the right information to get it to where God intends. My spirit was recreated with the Spirit of God, but my mind was messed up from the past. The degree to which I fed on the Word of God was the degree my mind was renewed, and no more. I held on to different things for all the wrong reasons, until I got to know the Word of God as a purifier to cleanse and renew my mind. On several nights, I would fall on my face and just talk to God, seeking Him in peace and quietness. All I wanted was to yield totally to Him, to live the life acceptable unto Him[5] and move to deeper heights and realms in my relationship with Him. These were my heart's deep-seated desires, but desire alone was most definitely not enough. I had such conflict within that I had to get past to truly anchor on Him.

Looking at all the confusion in my mind, I became tired of trying. Walking with God is much more than an instantaneous relationship. I knew the time had to come to walk in His freedom and pull down all the strongholds on my mind. Stability in my relationship with the Holy Ghost and in the Word of God became a reality when I took advantage of His presence. As I began studying the Word, I realized that I needed to renew my mind with the Word of God *"...for they are life to those who find them, and health to all their flesh."*[6] The mind is the battlefield where all our desires conflict with the things of God, so it had to be brought under the Holy Ghost's control. I could move to new levels in my relationship with God because I medicated whatever came my way with the Word and His presence. I confronted the real issues that threatened my sanity and gave them up to the Lord.

Before then, the anointing of God could not operate in my life because I had the form of God, but my life denied its godliness: only for the simple reason that I had not completely yielded my all to Him. I discovered that the anointing of God couldn't operate outside the Word of God. The Word of God activates the anointing. Wanting the anointing of God's burden-removing, yoke-destroying power to be operative in my life was a far cry when I did not make His presence priority. It dawned on me that I had to lay the Word in my heart, like the psalmist said, *"Your word have I hidden in my heart that I might not sin against you."*[7]

When your spirit is dead to the things of God, and you are filled with all manners of unrighteousness,[8] God cannot accomplish much through you. He is Holy and will not use you fully, if you habitually live by doing whatever you choose to do. He has given you His nature of holiness in your spirit, so therefore you must yield yourself to Him. If you will forsake your ways and come to Him, He is faithful and just to forgive you and cleanse you from all unrighteousness. Not only that, He will also set you on the right path. I had my struggles because I was not completely yielded to Him. As long as I remained unbroken and unyielded to God, I denied Him control and a relationship built upon submission and trust. The time I kept a part of me to myself made it completely difficult for us to walk together. For two to walk together is nearly impossible if they do not agree.[9]

For as long as I did not hand over lordship of my life to Him and die to my carnal appetites by the enabling of the Holy Ghost, the Lord could do nothing to ease my pains and satisfy my heart's longing. I lacked the peace of God because my flesh kept warring against the Spirit of God that dwelt in me. Talk about the highest level of carnality. The things I laid up at the altar when I received Christ kept springing up because my walk with God was inconsistent. I was constantly bitter and unhappy because two masters were warring inside me and I gave into both. No man can serve two masters. You cannot be cold and hot at the same time; you are either one or the other. If you are inconsistent, how do you receive the things that God has freely given your spirit man?

You see, I began to isolate myself and timidity began to take a royal seat in my life. What was I missing out on? How could I be so timid when Scripture declares *"...the righteous is bold as a lion."* [10] I spent so much unproductive time by myself that I became inhibited. (Believe me, that the unproductive mind is an unfruitful mind: its typical of the fig tree cursed by Jesus. The tree stood tall and strong, yet remained unproductive and, consequently, unfruitful. To avoid unfruitfulness, you must be planted in the right environment in life.) Taking a Taylor Johnson's Temperament Test[11] revealed the inhibitive trait within me. Such inhibition is not from God and is certainly not an encouraging trait: the inhibited individual is unable to show warm feelings, stays sensitively guarded, and has a tendency for reserve so as to maintain control. Some may also appear insensitive or even withdrawn. In many cases, this disposition causes problems in one's relationships.

What did I need all that negativity for when I am created in the image and likeness of God? When I came to a point of self-realization, I understood full well what the enemy was after. In my spirit, I was upset about these test results. I made up my mind to find out what God's word had to say about me instead and then walk in the reality of that Word. To counteract that inhibitive trait within me, I got into the Word to find the truth about who God says I am. I can tell you that the Word works. If you apply the Word of God over the issues in your life, you are destined for greatness. When the devil can isolate your mind from that living truth, he will feed you with junk from the pit of hell: such as lies about how alone you are, and how no one in the world cares for you.

When the devil has you right where he wants you—that is, alone in fear and timidity— he is set to destroy you. I found that to be true while studying the story of the madman in the tomb at Gadara.[12] Picture this image in your mind: a son of the Most High God living in a tomb and having relationship with dead things! The devil had this man bound up in isolation. The man spent his days in the tomb wasting life on issues, circumstances and relationships long dead and buried. He could not come to terms with personal issues that needed to be released. He held onto what should have given them to God. The past's unresolved, dead-and-buried issues caused him to become angry and destructive. The end result left him with a very poor self-image and a distorted picture of self.

Without knowledge of who you really are, life becomes cold and ugly. What's more is that this strong man had a temper beyond control. It is tragic that a normal, healthy functional man will leave his home and move to the tombs to take up residence with dead issues. This happened because he allowed his personal issues to take control. This man even began cutting himself all over his body—talk about out-of-control anger and a low sense of worth. Such self-destructive behaviors are red flags that point to isolation. When you begin to feel anger due to lack-of-control of what's happening around you, you are denying the truth of your existence because you cannot come to terms with what you see.

Watch out for these signs of isolation. You become isolated when you leave home, and that means whatever home represents for you. For all intents and purposes, this absence from home is not just in the physical sense. When you feel yourself fleeing emotionally or mentally, that is the time to slam on brakes and pray. When your temper rages beyond control, that is a time to take heed, search the Scriptures and pray.

The devil is such a liar! His only agenda is to kill, steal and destroy. He is always on the lookout, targeting areas of your life that he can conquer. When you are dealing with issues; an inability to trust wholeheartedly will cause you to withdraw into a shell and become suspicious of people. I was once suspicious of every move anyone made towards me. All that suspicion was the enemy's to get me into an isolated state of mind. At that time, I had not fully absorbed such spiritual truths as, "I am more than a conqueror. The greater one lives inside me and that I am the head and not the tail." I built a wall around me that kept everyone at bay. I worked so hard so that I could take care of myself and pay my bills. In itself, this goal is not wrong. But it becomes a different matter all together when you begin to idolize self and base your life's standard on material acquisition. I was dependent on self due to my fear of an unknown tomorrow. When you don't put trust in the Holy Ghost who is your Helper, then you will build your own security systems. Any self-support security is one built on the arm-of-the-flesh and, sad to say, that will fail you every time.

Although I cannot explain how this happened, one day everything came crashing in on me because I had built my security upon self. Strangely enough, the harder I worked, the more difficult life became. I realized that I needed to get my attention on the things above and truly seek first the Kingdom of God and His righteousness.

So began my journey of walking with God, waiting in His presence and trusting Him for every need. One time, I was so broke that I could not afford sanitary towels for my time of the month. Now I knew that was a serious issue. But no matter how bad my circumstances looked, I made up my mind to stay within the boundary where God's love would reach me. (His desire is for us to walk in the abundance that He has provided. If you are lack that right now, His will is for you to be filled up.)

I refused to compromise the joy of His presence no matter how tough life became. I trusted Him despite the pressures I faced, and He came through for me then and many times over. I stayed with the Word and found out that I had walked from the realm of His provision to one of blessings. I have since come to know Him as Jehovah Jireh, "my provider" and Jehovah El-shaddai, "my all sufficient God." He had to get me to stop depending on people, resources and my ability to do anything for myself. I have watched him heal my broken heart and put my discombobulated emotions back together. I am in my right mind, and that is "the mind of Christ."

The greatest encouragement I have gotten in this life is the Word of God. (I am not going about seeking help from those who can't even help themselves.) God brought me back from the brink of despair and frustration. When the chips were down, I encouraged myself in the Lord. No one can do a better job at encouraging yourself than you can. No matter how bad your situation gets, there is a future, a hope and a certainty in the Lord. Take that situation that threatens your peace and speak life to it in His presence. God brought me from miry clay to a solid foundation. I may never know your story, so I write to introduce you to the One not only knows your story, but stands with an outstretched arms beckoning you to hand over all to Him. Take that first step and see what He will do to break chains that have kept you in bondage.

It Does Not Matter Who or What...

Your issues may hurt terribly, but there is a higher way of life in the God's presence. His is the way of power and dominion over the wiles and stratagems of the enemy. His path is the way up in the valley of "dry bones." It does not matter who left you, through rejection or death, and is never coming back; it does not matter who violated your purity and ran off only for you to become pregnant with a child from rape, a few months later; and it does not matter who lied on you either. I realize that all these situations, and the ever-increasing list of life's turbulences, come with pain. Most times we feel hurt when badly treated or unjustly handled by moments in life. But with Jesus, your life is different story altogether. You can't just sit down and let anything happen to you. Instead, you have to make things happen yourself. So get up from your comfort zone, pray and believe Him. If you believe on Him, rivers of living water will flow from your belly. In life, you prevail on your knees. What's going to get you beyond your issues in life is intimate time with Him. When you spend time praying, changes begin to happen.

So many times I have had to deal with issues: I know that you can't sit still and watch life pass you by and hope change will come. You have to make the change happen. A dear brother of mine went home to be with the Lord at a tender age. Later on, my father also made his journey to Heaven. The circumstances surrounding their deaths cut deeply into my heart. After he suffered from diabetes, I saw my father take a detour in life in the clutching hands of death. His passing was exceptionally painful because I had to watch my once energetic father go from one insulin injection to another, until he ended up on the dialysis machine for months, then the respiratory machine and, ultimately, his death.

Standing in a cold hospital room and watching Dad die, with nothing I could do to help, is my definition of helplessness and pain. Where was the faith for his healing? How come he didn't come out of it alive? As tough as the answers were, suffice it to say that "faith is not faith until it is faith." What do I mean by this? The Scriptures make us understand that if we just speak for the mountain to be removed and cast into the sea and do not doubt in our hearts, then we shall have what we say. I said all sorts of confessions, but did I really believe that Dad would rise up and walk again? Days turned into weeks and then months, but Dad's condition just grew worse. On a Sunday morning, I held him and watched him breath his last. At that moment, in that cold hospital room lacking any comfort, I looked into my mother's eyes and knew that life is just a stage we pass through. If we are not waiting on the Creator of the heavens and the earth, then what are we doing?

After Dad passed on, I readjusted my focus and got a clearer understanding that if life didn't work out how I had imagined, then there must be a better way of handling issues. God will never inflict pain on us to draw us closer to Him, and we are never alone when we have challenges. A higher law at work places us above the intimidation of life's trials. Know that in the midst of your turmoil and distress, sickness and sorrow, the sun of righteousness will arise with healing in His wings[13] on your behalf. Again, it does not matter what pressures you are going through now. What does matter is that God is knocking at the door of your heart. He wants to enter in so as to sooth your pain, put a smile on your face again and turn your mourning into dancing. He specializes in mending broken hearts, so that He can give you hope where you feel hopeless.

One sunny Saturday afternoon, I received a phone call that a mob act broke out in Jostown, and our family home had been set ablaze. The apartment was completely burnt to ashes. As soon as we could, Frank and I rushed home to see for ourselves and be with mother, whose home had just been torched. I stood speechless for a while, but amidst all the nagging questions on my mind, I felt the Holy Spirit's gentle touch remind me about the peace of God in life's crisis. My thoughts immediately went to my mother. Later on in the day, I had an opportunity to speak with her. I wanted to know how she felt in the midst of everything. She said to me, "Look, Lami, what is most important to me now is the fact that I was not caught in that fire. I can live yet another day to declare the goodness of the Lord in the land of the living."

We all have trials and test that spring up when we least expect them. But whether the loss is your home, a loved one or your own identity, God remains faithful through it all. He will hold you with His warmth in the crisis of life. Because His grace is sufficient, His goodness and faithfulness will cause you to see dawn after the darkest experience in your life. You may go through the fire of life's experiences, but you will not be burnt. As long you hold on to Him with an unchanging heart, His touch has enough power to bring to life into what had been written off for dead. Almighty God lives right inside you and has given you the authority over the issues of life, so it is possible to take charge of circumstances and boldly declare your goals. If you do not activate that power, you will constantly live in defeat. It is time to rise above all the devil's lies and deceptions, and take authority over your sphere of influence because greatness and His ability are living inside you.

Clearly Defined Boundaries

God's in-dwelling presence has given you power and dominion over sin. Sin can never be a stronghold in your life because God's nature lives in you. If you are born of God, the seed of God dwells in you. First John 3:9 clearly shows us that *"whosoever is born of God doth not sin; for his seed remaineth in him: and he cannot sin because he is born of God."* Knowing what God speaks about sin is very expedient for you in terms of walking in the wisdom of God's word. Even though the very nature of righteousness resides in your spirit, you must walk circumspect because we are living in evil days. In your walk of "waiting on the Lord," it is important to set clearly defined boundaries over issues, places and situations because God has a set standard for living. There are some experiences you cannot indulge because your body is the temple of the living God. He is Holy and to walk with Him, you must be set apart unto good works. When you come to saving knowledge of Christ, if you do not consciously decide to live a consecrated life, you will keep missing the mark of His high calling.

When Frank and I met, one boundary we did not waste time defining was in keeping the marriage bed undefiled. We knew God's heart concerning sex outside marriage, so we made the decision not violate that trust. A lot of people consider sexual sins to be a casual matter. Sex outside marriage is a trap from the enemy that cuts deep into the Father's heart because it pollutes a covenant relationship. Sin disconnects us from our source of life, so we cannot afford to be casual with sin. When you define boundaries in life, with the Holy Ghost's help, it is easy to walk circumspectly, as one who wisely follows the precepts of almighty God. Doing what you are supposed to do in accordance with the Word does not leave an occasion for you to stumble and fall. Even when challenges present themselves, He has already made a way-of-escape. When you search the Word, you will find escape routes hidden in the secret treasures of His presence.

Before getting married, Frank and I needed to present to our premarital counselors with results of an HIV test. The night before going for the test, I sat on my bed thinking, "There is only a thin line between life and its flip side: death." In the twinkle of an eye, everything can either go so right or so wrong depending on your past choices. As a child of God, there are some things you cannot touch, people you cannot hang out with and places you cannot make a habitual dwelling place so as not to disrespect the anointing. I thought of the story I once read of a boy dying from AIDS at the age of 12. At that moment, I thought life was terribly unfair. So I said, "God, there are some things I do not understand." Please talk to my heart. Why should the innocent boy suffer this?" Here comes His answer: "Bad things do come against good people who do not know their rights and inheritance in Christ, but there is nothing you cannot change on your knees and by the power of God vested upon your life."

You must make a conscious decision to search the Word yourself and discover the promises of life. The people of God perish because of lack of knowledge. Let the anointing go ahead of you and illuminate your path. If you search for Him, you will definitely find Him. Life offers you choices consistently, sort of like the stem of a rose flower! Can you understand why just below the beautiful rose petals sit thorns on its stem? You chose which of the two you want to fix your gaze upon. Appreciate the colorful scented petals and enjoy the beauty and freshness in life, or stare at the thorns that prick hearts and leave people bleeding.

While life offers its own choices— and, truthfully, you might not be able to do much about them without power from the Holy Ghost—what choices are you making on your own? Who do you hang out with who you shouldn't be? What are you doing now that you ought not to be doing? While God is working in you a far exceeding weight of glory, you must stay within that boundary where His love can reach you. I was tempted to wish I never made some of my choices, but as I retraced my steps back to God, I have come to know peace. Those setbacks became translated into many things that worked out for my good. I had to know that I was not just going to come to the altar, say the Sinner's Prayer and—presto—everything was changed. I had to go through a Holy Spirit schooling and allow Him train my mind; He removed all that junk I fed it while I lived life without Him, and set plans and goals without His signature endorsed on my life. I had to get the Word into my heart daily, because it holds all the transforming power.

Sex Sins: A Trap for Transfer of Spirits

I am not listing sins to condemn you, because there is no condemnation if you are in Christ. In talking about boundaries, sexuality is one boundary that must be set over your life. Your vessel is honorable before God and He wants us to maintain it that way. The issue of sex sins is not altogether strange. The only reason you don't hear about it is for the simple reason that many do not think it should be mentioned in the congregation of the saints. "We have brought our untamed passions under the Word," many saints say. But behind closed doors, these very same people have issues to deal with. Right in the middle of sharing about "waiting on the Lord," I spring up with the issue of sex sins. You are, no doubt, wondering, "What on earth is she up to and where is she going?"

The enemy has perverted certain truths, but if we get a hold of these truths in our spirit, there is no level of intimacy we cannot attain with our Father God. The only way to get right is to expose the evil one's hidden agenda. In the context of marriage, sex is good and honorable. It is spiritual act symbolic of worship, with an exchange of pleasure for satisfaction—like the intimacy in worship experience between our spirit man and Almighty God. In His presence is fullness of joy and, at His right hand, pleasures forever more. We receive His pleasure in our spirit, soul and body as we give Him satisfaction in pleasurable worship.

Much has gone wrong with the whole sex issue because its purity and holiness has been perverted. Many people are hung up on adultery, fornication, homosexuality, lesbianism, bestiality and the list goes on. Sex is a spiritual act, so it carries severe consequences outside the institution of marriage. In trading the joy of His presence and our covenant relationship with Him for idols in our lives, we are setting ourselves up for destruction. He will not share His glory with any man, so boundaries must be set in our love relationship with Him.

It is crucial that child of God sets boundaries, because the enemy is out to get you at all costs. When you engage in casual sex, you take on the spirit of the one whom you are sleeping with. If you have sex with 10 different people in one week, for instance, you take 10 different spirits into your own. Sometimes you begin to manifest varying degree of strange behaviors and many nasty things begin to happen to you, which cannot be explained. You are now trapped with other spirits that will keep you bound until you yield that sexual appetite to a purging of the Holy Ghost. You must set boundaries to keep yourself pure. Your body is the temple of the living God, so you must worship Him in spirit and in the reality of who He is. The Holy God does not behold iniquity.

But what do you do when your spirit is laced up with many other strange spirits? As long as your spirit is wrapped in bedroom sheets that are not yours, forget about successfully waiting on God. If other people's bedroom sheets have bound you, the Holy Spirit is calling you to come out of those sheets right now. He is waiting on you to reach Him just the way you are. For those whom the devil has bound up with his sex traps, I particularly recommend *No More Sheets*[14] by Juanita Bynum.

Sex is one stronghold the devil has used to keep many from getting into the presence of the Most High God; he has done so by filling them with much dread, guilt and condemnation. In the real sense, casual sex is only a manifestation of deeper spiritual issues. Sex outside the marriage covenant is used to sooth the pain and fill the void of inner emptiness. Unless the Lord fills up that void, you will only continue to take in more layers of strange spirits. God has placed so much value on you. How dare you make light of your intrinsic worth and value in Christ by engaging in casual sex? It is all a trap, and the Lord wants to set you free from that yoke of bondage. You can never know deep levels of intimacy unless you present yourself to Him as a living sacrifice. If you will let Him, the Holy Spirit will do a thorough work in you.

Beyond the Prayer Line

I soaked my spirit with the Word of God on a daily basis. I didn't get delivered just by staying in the prayer line. Staying in the prayer line is good, if it works for you. But, quite frankly, I needed more than the prayer line. I had to get the Word into my heart and travail in prayer for myself. At times, I almost gave up because I felt like nothing was adding up. Other times, it became a challenge not to cross all those already defined boundaries. But as I refused to be struck with amazement over situations staring me in the face, I watched a transformation come upon my life. The transition was one of victory into Christ Jesus.

In all honesty, when I walked out of darkness into God's light, I went through unadulterated pressures, but I had a firm resolve concerning my relationship with Him. I knew that God had already won the battle, but I had to do what was most needed and stay at the Master's feet and learn of Him. I would lay flat on my face seeking His face. As I sought His face in prayer and in the Word, he quickened my life. I began to walk in that newness of life where you move from lack to abundance, from the miry clay to a solid foundation and from not-enough to more-than-enough in your spirit, soul and body. I got myself back on track, tasted the love of God, and began to walk in His healing power and comfort. All I wanted was more of Him; all I still ever want is more of Him. I disciplined myself to delay gratification and wait on Him. I decided within me to live a life of contribution. I was only going to go up in my relationship with God, and was determined in my spirit not to go back to Egypt because any road to the past left behind is a move of downward motion. I had only one motion in perspective—the upward, forward motion—which is a higher calling in Christ Jesus.

Having made this decision to be committed to my course, I have watched God steadily turn my life around. I have seen Him restore my name and give me dignity. He took away the shame and reproach of my youth and made me an heir of salvation. I heard the Holy Spirit gently remind me that *"...we overcame him by the blood of the lamb and by the word of our testimony."*[15] Yes, I quite agree that most of what I have shared so far is not what most people readily want to discuss, or even admit to for that matter, for fear of criticism. While living in sin, there is nothing cute about what anyone does. As for me, now that I have tasted God's goodness and what He has done for me, I can't keep quiet. The Holy Ghost did major surgery on me. If the Lord had not been on my side, where would I be? Believe me, if the Lord is not on your side, then you will not get very far in life.

ENDNOTES

1. Matthew 11:28
2. Jeremiah 29:11
3. John 4:24
4. 2 Corinthians 5:17
5. Romans 12:1
6. Proverbs 4:22
7. Psalm 119:11
8. Romans 1:29-32
9. Amos 3:3
10. Proverbs 28:1
11. Taylor Johnson's Temperament test (Copyright 1995, 1997) Psychological Publication, Inc., P.O. Box 3577, Thousand Oaks, CA 91359-0577
12. Mark 5:1-15 KJV
13. Malachi 4:2
14. Juanita Bynum. (*No More Sheets*. Pnuema Life Publishing, P.O. Box 885, Lanham, MD 20703)
15. Revelation 12:11 AMP

Soul Search

1. Look deep within your heart and tell yourself the truth no one else would. What co-dependent relationship(s) are you involved with that you know you shouldn't be? Do you want to be completely free from it/them?

2. With the help of the Holy Spirit, what boundaries do you need to set for yourself?

3. What are those things that might become hindrances to setting the boundaries in your life?

4. Are you caught up in any sexual traps, even if it only relates to your imagination? What are these traps and how do you intend on dealing with them?

CHAPTER 2

When Emptiness and Unfulfillment Strike

I had a longing and a thirst for God. Within me, I sensed that He was about to do something in my life. I felt His touch upon me and knew that I was destined for greatness in the Kingdom. I had knew that He translated me from the domain of darkness into His marvelous light for a purpose: therefore, there was no vacuum in my life that He could not fill. I came to understand that when you start out with God, it is by one step at a time until you come into the fullness of His plan for your life. I was determined to stay within the boundary where God's love would always reach me. Daily, I began to realize that every level with God had lessons to be learnt and new heights to walk in. I opened up my heart to go through training with the Holy Ghost. I needed to allow Him to retrain me, create in me a new heart and renew the right spirit within me.

Gradually, I came to the point—without realizing it—where all the deposits from past carnal relationships I had had been in were laid off me by the Holy Ghost, and I didn't even know how. All I knew was that I felt extremely lonely at times, but amidst all the loneliness, I understood that He needed my attention. Without Him, nothing I touched was of significance to my fulfillment in life. Only God could fill that vacuum within me. Then I realized that if I was ever going to get anywhere with God, I needed to let Him touch me: the only way of doing this was to continually wait in His presence.

I also realized that just coming to God was not enough. I needed to abide in His presence. In the Scriptures, He said, with amazing clarity and brevity, *"If anyone does not abide in Me, he is cast out as a branch and is withered; and men gather them and cast them into the fire, and they are burned."*[1] As I lingered in His presence, I began to experience real peace: I had renewed strength to walk through pressures; and I could boldly look at friends I used to hang out with and tell them about the new man in my spirit. As I watched Him process me and lead me daily in His path, my life took an amazing turn. Without Him, life is a constant battle. You may be doing a lot of things without Him right now, and you are lonely. Striving so hard to fit into the status quo, you are tired of trying and falling all the way: that failure is because He is not involved in what you are doing. The simple answer is that "He needs to get your attention."

Let Him Step into The Emptiness

> *From the beginning of creation, at various times God has spoken in diverse ways and in these last days, through his son Jesus Christ.*[2]

He is trying to get your attention because what you need is right there is His presence. You must be sensitive enough to hear Him calling out to you. God could be speaking to you in diverse ways. But He may never get your attention if you are too busy and inundated with "life" and its never-ending list of priorities. You may be so engulfed with yourself—and all those things in your life that are not adding up—that you cannot respond to Him. You are inundated with pain, pressure, distress and activities that cluster your mind. Bound by your own actions from past tragedies, you don't see a way out of the tunnel you have found yourself in. The resulting effects of all your "issues" have left you lonely, broken, empty, and dysfunctional. You have done all within your power to fill the vacuum inside, but alas, you remain empty.

Can I be real with you? There is no way out of whatever situation you find yourself in, except when you turn and wait on Him. Waiting on the Lord is not a quick fix, and you should not come to Him with a hidden agenda either. Just come the way you are and, if you are sincere, everything else will be sorted out. Realize that nothing remains hidden before the Lord God. He created all things and only in Him that can we truly live, move and have our being. Coming to God is one matter. Staying fixed in His presence is another matter entirely. In John 15:7, He said, *"If you abide in me and my words abide in you, ye shall ask what ye will, and it shall be done unto you."* With clarity, this verse speaks about a relationship. Waiting on Him is indicative of a love relationship.

"Waiting" is going to cost you faithfulness, obedience and commitment. These three qualities do not happen over night, but are a process you begin and stay with until you enter His rest. In the days of old, Isaac did what did not feel comfortable. He obeyed God and sowed in the land of famine because the Lord told Him to do so. As he sowed, he began the process of prospering, and continued to prosper until he became a very prosperous man.[3] When you faithfully wait on Him, your situation will begin to change, and continue to change until it comes to a glorious end. I can assure you that faithfulness is not a fly-by-night affair. You have to continue in fellowship with God and His kingdom way of doing things. Keep a forward momentum on His ways to experience real rest from the dead works in your life and have the peace of God that surpasses all understanding. God wants you to come just as you are. Don't waste time trying to fix yourself because you cannot fix a thing.

Oh, how I tried to get myself together before going to Him. I thought I could clean up after my addictions and then find my way to Him, but that process never worked. How do you begin to fix a broken heart? How do you mend a heart raped of the love it once knew? How do you free yourself from all the guilt ripping you apart every time you have flashbacks of all those issues you were once involved in? Where do you begin when you have tried to stop the drugs, alcohol, rape, bestiality, homosexuality, lesbianism, abortions, killings, stealing and other activities on the endless list. Church folks do not like to talk about these dead works, but they do exist amongst us and they are ripping the Church apart.

You are not just going to come to the altar and recite the Sinner's Prayer and then be good-to-go. No way! These issues are an overflow of more, deep-rooted problems and have to be dealt with in God's presence. These deep issues stem from an intense need for God, which you might be unaware of due to a clouded mind. He alone knows what you are truly going through, with those secrets that keep you awake at night as uncontrollable tears wet your pillows. You struggle, but dare not mention these issues outside because it is taboo to do so. Everyone expects you to be "okay" on the outside and continue looking dignified. But you know about the mass of decay on your inside. Why do you hold onto "the image" and live such a painful, discombobulated life? Now this is not a judgmental message, but how can you ever experience the joy His presence brings if you are "together" on the outside yet so "out of place" on the inside. You are dying slowly. The enemy has got you terribly bound. Why are you being cute with that? Why won't you come to God just the way you are?

The madman at the Gadarenes tomb had demons right to the very core of His being, but He came to Jesus the way he was. The man fell at the Master's feet and worshipped Him. For many people, the deeper issues of life do not matter as long as you look clean, smell nice and fit in to the "acceptable circle." But you know that inside you are a mess. Your lifestyle stinks and you are sinking into the abbeys of self-destruction. Listen to me, God wants you to know that there is hope. Stop being cute with your issues, and quit pretending that everything is okay just because you look so dignified. He will take your battered self, wash you clean and fill you with His anointing and power. Until you hand over complete control of your life to Him, you are not going to have a release of joy, peace and righteousness in the Holy Ghost and freedom from all that pressure. To experience change in that situation, you must let Him step into that whatever emptiness you find yourself in.

He Will Fill the Empty Net

There is therefore now no condemnation to those who are in Christ Jesus who do not walk according to the flesh, but according to the Spirit. [4]

The Word is now, not tomorrow or next year, but now! If you handover your life to the leading of the Almighty God's Spirit, there is absolutely no way your life can remain the same. If you just make it to Him now and allow yourself to be led by the Spirit, you will be amazed at the difference. I had failed in many areas of my life and then realized that, without Him, my life was quickly passing me by. The more days that went by, the emptier I became until I handed over lordship of my life to Him. I want to share an insight from Scripture about Simon Peter that completely revolutionized my life and made it so obvious that I needed God more than anyone else. I had gotten to the point where nothing else mattered to me except Him. I was completely desperate for Him when I came across this passage that completely changed my life.

> *So it was, as the multitude pressed about Him to hear the word of God that he stood by the Lake Gennesaret, and saw two boats standing by the lake; but the fishermen had gone from them and were washing their nets. Then he got into one of the boats, which was Simon's, and asked him to put out a little from the land. And he sat down and taught the multitudes from the boat. When he had stopped speaking, he said to Simon, "Launch out into the deep and let down your nets for a catch." But Simon answered and said to Him, "Master, we have toiled all night caught nothing: nevertheless, at your word I will let the net." And when they had done this, they caught a great number of fish, and their net was breaking. So they signaled to their partners in the other boat to come and help them and they came and filled boats, so that they began to sink. When Simon Peter saw this, he fell down at Jesus knees, saying "Depart from me, for I am a sinful man, O Lord!"* [5]

Simon Peter had spent all night toiling, using whatever energy his own strength could muster. What was he doing? He was out with a net searching to catch fish, but, to his dismay, his nets remained empty. Casting their life's net in all the wrong directions seems to be the lifestyle of many people today. You have spent all your time and energy trying to make ends meet. You are busy trying to clean up your messed-up life and straighten out decisions that cost you peace and happiness. But even then, you come out empty and dissatisfied. At the end of all this toil, you are just as empty as Peter's net. He thought he knew what to do: he had a boat and a net, but he had no Jesus in his boat. Peter's situation did not change until Jesus stepped into his boat. As long as the Lord is not with you, you will be empty on all sides. You will never know true happiness and fulfillment. You will try your hands on many things, casting your net in the wrong directions of life, but never ever finding a real sense of fulfillment.

I recalled that I had cast my life's net everywhere. I let down nets under sheets, in controlled substances, on my job, on money, and more money, and in parties and clubs. But at the end of the day, I was very distraught and had nothing to show for my efforts. I only had a desperate cry within for real satisfaction. Many people today are just as dissatisfied and disoriented. They are empty and pressed on many sides because they have not allowed the Lord's presence into their life's journey. They have everything they think they need, except for the most important person: the Lord Jesus Christ.

All things may pacify you, but only His presence will ever satisfy you. You may even succeed in some things you lay your hand to do: climbing the success ladder; getting to the peak of your career; owning the most expensive houses; buying expensive cars and, generally, enjoying "the good life." That list of so-called perks is inexhaustible. Most of them are not wrong, in themselves, and acquiring them is certainly no big deal. Our God owns the cattle on a thousand hills, so why not enjoy life in Him? But setting material acquisition and soulish gratification as life's standard is very wrong in deed. Things of this world just don't bring fulfillment. Nothing but God's presence, and an eternal relationship with Him, brings real satisfaction.

A few years ago, a couple of days before my birthday, I made a list of everything I wanted, including a party to put a cap on the day. I swung into action, got every single item I had listed to amuse myself with, invited all the people I wanted and had my party. The house was flooded with people and we partied the evening out. I went to bed, only to awaken in tears the next day. I felt so alone. Where were all the people? I looked at all my possessions—the jewelry, expensive clothes, shoes, wristwatches and bags—and I became more miserable and angry because something was definitely missing. I thought to myself, "Is that all there is to life?" Certainly, there had to be more to life than all this.

Remember Peter's emptiness was toiling hard all night with nothing to show for it. He had no catch of life's promises, achievements and goals! All he got after a hard day's work was a lack of peace, contentment and frustration. But one day, he had an encounter with the Lord Jesus Christ, and met face-to-face with the One who knows the solutions to life's challenges. Jesus reached out to Peter, who listened and obeyed what He told him to do. Afterwards, Peter's life was never the same. When I saw that for myself, I knew that handing my all-in-all to him was the only wise choice to make.

Today, I introduce to you the Master Fisher, the One who will teach you how to catch true, godly fulfillment to life's dreams. Just like the Lord told Simon Peter, *"cast the net of your life into his presence."* The moment Peter obeyed, his situation changed. He enjoyed a net-breaking, boat-sinking catch of fish. Peter was so awestruck that he fell on his knees and cried out to Jesus. Right now, you may be like Peter in certain areas of life. What you need to do right away is hand over that empty net of your life to Him and watch Him fill it up with His Glory. He is about to do a work that will make you fall on your knees and acknowledge His Lordship.

When Peter trusted God to the point that He handed over everything to Him, his life turned out just as the psalmist wrote, that *"When the Lord brought back the captivity of Zion, it was like those who dreamed."*[6] The turn-around in Peter's circumstance was a wonder to him. He saw his own desperation and realized that refusing to yield to Jesus would have prevented him from receiving a touch of the miraculous. The same will happen to you when you let Him in to your situation. If you are looking for peace, He will give to you peace because He is the "prince of peace." If the laughter in your life has dried up or was never there in the first place, he will be laughter to you because "the joy of the Lord is your strength." Are you mentally, physically or emotionally sick, whatever you need is in His total package of salvation.

Cooperate with the Holy Ghost

Earlier in this chapter, I shared that God spoke in diverse ways, in time past through his prophets and has in these last days spoken to us by his Son. Because He is the same yesterday, today and forever, He is still speaking to us in diverse ways and through his Son Jesus Christ who is the living Word. But what He is saying will not work if you don't cooperate with the Holy Ghost. You must allow Him lead you, guide you, walk with you and be your direction in life. He alone can lead you from the beginning of life's journey so that you can grow into the fullness of God's ordained life for you. Like Isaiah said, He is our wonderful counselor. If we gave Him first place in our heart, we wouldn't need all these different types of counselors. He will be all we desire because He is here with us and He dwells in us.

You are a Son of God, if you allow the Holy Spirit to lead you.[7] This leading should become your lifestyle. It is not a gamble you play with your life, but a daily walk you engage in as you yield to the Holy Ghost. You cannot be lead by the Holy Ghost, when a multitude of things compete for His attention and you refuse to relinquish control of your life. You cannot be lead by the Holy Ghost when you are so involved with life that your heart has no place left for Him. When you do not spend time with God, you can never really get Him involved with your life issues.

A realm of knowing and hearing Him is restricted from those who do not submit to His control and entrust their lives to wait on Him. You cannot hear God when your mind is heavy with the pressures and weights of daily living. Look inward for all those things that blur your perception of God's direction and purpose for your life. You may be asking yourself right now, "What is that makes communion with the Holy Ghost so difficult?" Looking at these profound Scriptures, we can see why so many people are stuck in life's journey. *"Therefore we also, since we are surrounded by so great cloud of witness, let us lay aside every weight, and the sin, which so easily ensnares us, and let us run with endurance the race that is set before us."* [8]

> *Now the works of the flesh are evident, which are adultery, fornication, uncleanness, lewdness, idolatry, sorcery, hatred, contentions, jealousy, outburst of wrath, selfish ambitions, dissensions, heresies, murders, drunkenness, revelries, and the like; which I tell you before hand, just as I also told in time past, that those who practice such things will not inherit the kingdom of God.* [9]

Realize that what the above Scriptures mention will pose as barriers to your relationship with the Holy Ghost. The time has come to do a self-analysis as to where you are in your walk with God. You need to find out what is responsible for your level of involvement with Him. Take a walk through life's pictures, and explore areas where you may have missed the mark or gotten a bad deal from life. You may find yourself lost in any one of these issues or more, but now is not the time for a pity party. When Jesus hung, bled and died from the cross at Calvary, he assumed all the world's pain, heartache, sickness, lack and diseases. Know that you don't have to through anything for which He already paid the price. Whatever your "moments" may represent, now is the time to cooperate with the Holy Spirit and work towards breakthrough because there is liberty in God's presence. As you yield yourself completely to Christ's atoning work at Calvary—and lay down all those sins and weights before Him—healing will come in whatever area you desire.

What Moments Did the Pictures of Your Life Catch?

Stored up in your memory are pictures of what you have done and wished you never did. Somewhere deep down lay pictures of what has happened to leave you broken and hopeless. You may have suffered many negative responses after being left heartbroken by someone who you thought you were going to share your life with. These experiences have been painful, and the unforgiveness, bitterness, malice and anger stored within have left you dysfunctional. Or maybe the issue is the fact that your spouse has turned home into a "center for abuse." You got the wrong deal, which has caused you untold unhappiness to the point of not being able to comprehend the depths of its emotional trauma. Out of desire to stay committed to your commitment, you choose not to leave. You consider the sacredness of your marriage vows and, all of a sudden, are torn in between two worlds.

Perhaps you are hooked on a codependent relationship, needing one drug to fall asleep and another one to wake up. It has gotten so bad that you are ashamed of yourself and do not know what to do. Then again, it may be that you don't know how it got to be that you constantly fall in and out of sexual sin. You hate continually falling into these traps, but you can't seem to stop yourself. The moment you finish consecrating yourself, you fall right back into the same trap. You are so hooked on pornography, and your mind so filthy with perversion that you can no longer think straight.

Is it the fact that your parents abandoned you as a child? You grew up never knowing true parental love? You spend your time lamenting over the fact that your identity is a crisis case! What exactly does life have to offer when your true identity remains a mystery? You were raped, bruised and battered! The rape has left you cold, indifferent, filled with hatred and promising to be vengeful and unfaithful in your marital relationship.

Talk about a dysfunctional mentality! Or maybe it's the unending series of abortions you have lost track of. You turned to the other side of your life and indulged in murder in cold blood. How bad can these moments get? Are you living with a sexually perverted spouse? You are sick-and-tired because it goes form one form of perversion to another: bestiality today and homosexuality tomorrow!

But I have a shocking revelation: the Lord loves you just the way you are. Your "moments" pale out in comparison to His unending love. These moments are certainly not for the purpose of condemnation, but to show you the pain, depravity and ineffectuality of a life without Christ. Whatever your case maybe—pain of rejection, emotional trauma, a lifestyle of sexual immorality, or unforgiveness—God is saying to you today, *"...forgetting those things that are behind...press towards the mark for the price of the high calling upon your life"* (Philippians 3:13,14). Simply "let go," and do it by the enabling of the Holy Ghost.

Walk in the newness of the life you have been called into. Get rid of the sin consciousness that has bound you up and walk in His light. Let go of all the besetting sin you have been carrying inside. Lay aside the weights by pursuing His presence. Turn away from what has kept you in bondage and turn to Him: He is faithful and just to forgive you and cleanse you from all unrighteousness. Distractions will stop you from running with endurance the race set before you. Violating God's marvelous precepts and perfect standard will hinder the progress of your relationship with Him and cause you to lose sight of His call upon your life. When you lay aside everything else to go after His presence, you will be refreshed.

Another side to life's moments has to do with your high-tension emotions, such as anger, rage, wrath, malice, and bitterness. Anger may have engulfed the very core of your existence, and you remain angry over what happened years ago. Quite frankly, some of these things should have buried and forgotten long ago. Rid yourself from whatever does not move eternity in Your life. Get to the point of telling yourself the truth of the Word, and consistently tell yourself what will set you free if you continue in the Lord. There is absolutely nothing you can do about what has already happened. So from that point on, look toward whatever way is forward. If you are very sincere, you will see the way out as you continue in the Word. God has gone ahead of you to make a way out, because He specializes in making ways where none seem to exist.

Dealing with the Root Cause of Your Issues

Sometimes, you will have to deal with the root cause of issues so as to move ahead. Many times, we sweep the dirt under the carpet because we are afraid to confront issues in our lives. Unfortunately, the more dirt we sweep under the carpet, the higher the carpet is raised from ground level and, eventually, that dirt has to come out. No matter how hard you try, you can't keep the dirt there neatly forever. After awhile, it elevates the carpet to a point of solid discomfort. That is just as true for issues left to the mercy of time and chance. Whatever issues are left unresolved will always spring up time and again to mess you up. That next time around could be a very painful experience that you don't want to endure. You will have to make a commitment to confront your issues in His presence.

When you can come to terms with all that has happened, or is perhaps still happening, you can then look at the problems' root causes, deal with them by the Holy Ghost's help and move on the way He intended. Some of you may need to stop buying filthy magazines and watching the dirty videotapes stocked in your libraries. Others will need to stop going to those parlors for full-body massages that end up grieving the Holy Ghost.

Some may need to a close a chapter of your life by confronting people who have hurt you. You may be saying, "If she only knew the depth of hurt caused me by this one person." This is true! I may not know who ran off with your spouse, got your only daughter pregnant, destroyed the business deal for you, or infected you with that terrible virus. While these issues may be hard to comprehend, you have to let go. Once you do that, it will be easy to allow God into your affairs so He can mend the cracks in your life. In putting you back together, He will make you realize that absolutely no one is worth the pangs of unforgiveness.

Simply put, you need to take responsibility for your life. God can do nothing for you if you keep going back to that filth. If you do not stop, you will be too far away from the boundary where His love can reach you. I must mention the important fact that you may have to drop certain relationships. This is where you must be spiritually sensitive. People are very important in our lives, but you cannot afford to keep certain relationships. No matter how hard you try to maintain them, some relationships are never going to be right. Be wary of people who waste your time, water down your values, and shift your focus from what God is trying to do in your life. He is taking you to an incredible height, which is why you have to stay focused on Him. When unresolved issues are dealt with and certain relationship boundaries drawn, you will feel very light in your spirit man. Then you can walk the path God has called you to without hindrance: a walk of abundant life and joy in the Holy Spirit.

Yearning for God will take you to great levels of relationship with Him. Experiencing and knowing the depth of God comes from quietness and stillness of His presence, which no human being can give.

Yearning Hard after God

As the dear pants for the water brooks, so pants my soul for you oh God. [10]

To discover hidden truths about God will take a yearning on your part. Lay aside all your pain, fear, frustration, loneliness, emptiness, and being brokenhearted to desperately yearn for Him. Let pursuit of a personal relationship with Him be an ultimate desire and your life will take a remarkable turn. Like the deer pants for streams of water, you need to pant for His presence. The deer pants for the waterbrook for two reasons: to satiate its thirst with water from the brook, and to find a hiding place from enemies by submerging itself into the water.

When you begin to yearn for your Creator, you will walk in the fullness of His presence as well as a peace that satisfies the longing human soul. He will fill the cracks in your life. He will become your hiding place from the devourers of life. He will become your refuge and shelter from destruction. Certain overwhelming situations may come against you, but they will not harm you. The past will no longer be a threat to you. Your emotions will not swing you back and forth, because your emotions are given over to His control. You will not desire to live in sin because tasting a different kind of relationship gives you a satisfaction that sin never could. There will be no need to walk in unforgiveness because experiencing His forgiveness shows you that unforgiveness can never birth God's will.

Under the Shadow of the Almighty

He who dwells in the secret place of the Most High shall abide under the shadow of the almighty.[11]

When you live under shelter of the Most High, you will find rest for your soul because everything pertaining to life and godliness is found in His presence. Before you can ever know what He has in store, you must spend time in His presence to find His direction for your life. Right now, you are probably in the wrong place, doing the wrong things, and mingling with the wrong set of people—all because you refused to settle some of life's past issues. Sometimes the past is not dealt with because it is so painful. You are afraid to confront moments of shame and disgrace, and people who have hurt and taken advantage of you. The reality of that past brings confusion, pain, distrust and hardness of heart.

You have come to the point of realizing that all the steps in your life have actually shaped who you are today. We may not know all things yet, but we do know what the Word says, *"that all things work together for the good of those who trust Him"* (Romans 8:28). You may even be in the right place, and doing the right things, but your mind is doing the wrong things. Sometimes, it is that "mind thing" that you don't want anyone to know about. You are tired of the mental filth, but you love His presence. Know that as long as you are under the shadow of the Almighty, those imaginations do not determine your identity because you are no ordinary person in Christ Jesus. You are not a strange personality. You are a unique and peculiar person[12] and, as long as you continue in the Word, your mind will be transformed.

God has placed value in you, and that value is the life of His Son Jesus Christ who shed His blood on your behalf for you to find fulfillment in life. Nothing compares to the blood Jesus Christ shed at Calvary, because that is the premium God placed on you before the foundation of world. You have greatness in you. You are destined for the top in life! In the eyes of the Father, you are somebody! You've got eternity down in your spirit. Until I went under His shadow, I used to be bent over and beat down from all the pressures of life, and I had low self-esteem. I had a "chicken" mentality: I was always so apologetic about everything until I discovered the eagle living within me. I have been soaring high even since and, believe me, the top is the best place to be. At the top, you will see like your Father sees. Everything is under your feet when you are at an altitude in His presence.

Now you may not know this, but you are so precious that He has chosen you to be His display board to the whole world. He wants to show His goodness to others through you. Quit seeing yourself as a failure and a weakling. Begin to walk in the reality of life that God has called you into. You may have been intimidated by the devil and you lack boldness to move an inch. You need boldness, strength, and confidence to bring whatever has tormented you before the throne of God: only there can you find rest for your weary soul. The Scripture has said to *"come boldly to the throne of Grace, that we may obtain mercy and find grace to help in time of need."*[13] When you can do that, you will find the strength to carry on. You will be free to walk and enjoy God as you move along life's path. Although it may not look so at the moment, the grace of God is sufficient for you at all times. Because you have been boxed-in on all sides by pressures, you may have even wondered if life is fair. But healing will come to you when you stay under the shadow of the Almighty. The enemy has desired to sift you out of God's plan, but he will not succeed. You cannot fail, because you are under the wings of God's grace.

I Thought Life Is Fair

You are wondering about life while in search of solutions to gnawing issues of life that people do not talk about. You do not consider these issues in life to be fair. You did not go out of your way to plan them, they just happened. You ask yourself, "What did I do to deserve all this?" What has happened in your life may not be fair, but hear this: God is fair to the point that He wants to touch you and right the wrongs of your life. Maybe you are confused about your life: your conception and birth may be the issue here. You are so ashamed of yourself because you cannot believe who your father is, or you do not even know who your father is. The scenario may be different, but the pain remains the same.

At different levels, the enemy tries us with different pressures. For some men, it is the quest to go up life's ladder-of-success mindless of the consequences. They work so hard night-and-day and have nothing to show for it. They toil endlessly, but are still unfulfilled. At the end of each day, they go home dissatisfied to their angry wives who see them as "less than able to achieve" because bills are not paid and needs are not met. Perhaps, someone told you that you are never going to amount to anything, and you believed those lies all your life.

You may be a single mother trying hard to raise the children all by yourself. (A very critical issue prevailing in our generation is that men must take responsibilities for children. You have fathered these sons and daughters, but have not been bold enough to live up to the consequences of your actions. Both of you may have moved on with your life, but the children are at the mercy of your actions. Men, take responsibility for your life and pay the child's bills! After all is said and done, you will gain respect with God.)

Or perhaps your self-esteem could be shattered by the effect of child abuse. Your father always sneaked into your room to sexually molest, but you could dare not say anything to your mother. Father made you promise to keep quiet and threatened punishment if you ever opened up your mouth. Now you're a grown woman tormented with the gory details of father's acts. You are cold and indifferent by past memories that won't let you go on. The list of life's thorny packages seems so unfair. Yes, life may not have been fair, but there is staying power in God's presence concerning your issues. Whatever the issue may be, you must go to the ultimate One who fulfills life. Otherwise, these issues will rob you of God-given dreams and visions. You must make a connection with the One who gives us power to trample over pressures and distractions.

Realizing that His presence is all that is needed will help you align your priorities with His and make the quest of His presence a primary focus. *"And he will give you all you need from day to day if you live for him and make the kingdom of God your primary concern."*[14] The New King James Version of the Bible says, *"but seek first the kingdom of God and His righteousness; and all these things shall be added unto you"* (Luke 12:31). It is such joy to make His kingdom your primary concern, by pursuing it daily. Aiming for the Kingdom of God means that your focus is on the Lord and what matters to Him. Now the issue is how to seek the Lord. It is important to know that God is God all by Himself. He is sovereign and majestic in His dealings, and He alone deserves all the glory from your life. I say this to let you know that your times are in His hands. Once you fully understand that truth, you need to pull away from everything else. Pursue Him with such tenacity like He is all you need to get to the next level in life, and, indeed, He is that.

Life Changes in His Presence

God is faithful and will do exactly what He says He will. When you have lost your strength, wait on Him. When life's experiences have taken you so low, and it seems as if there is no way out, wait on Him. When you can't find the energy to run in life's race any longer, wait on Him. When you are heavily yoked on all sides with life's burdens and cannot walk, wait on him. When you decide to become a better person and live a life that blesses other people, God will strengthen you to do what you never thought possible. You are designed to constantly wait on God. When you seek hard after God, He becomes your very essence for survival and you receive divine ability to live a life that goes beyond your expectations. You become a person of true worth and influence in the lives of others.

By ourselves, there isn't so much we can achieve. We are limited in our ability, but God's strength is perfected when we submit to His will. We lose strength when we do not wait on God. We cannot move to a higher level in our relationship with God because we are not waiting on Him. We cannot run the race of life He has called us to while heavy with cares and worries. We cannot walk when our spiritual knees are weak. When you wait on God, you are saying, "Father, I trust you to enable me serve You with my life, dedicating my life and time, energy and resources for the sake of the Kingdom."

Ministering to lost and needy souls becomes a delight. In waiting on the Lord, you will get to discover that He touches you so that you can touch someone else. You become a life-giver yourself since the Author of life dwells within you. Everything simply goes beyond you and your challenges. Again, as you wait on Him you are saying, "I trust You to get me out of this situation. I trust You to heal my broken heart, and to give me a plan and a strategy for my life. You are saying, "I know you have healed my spirit, soul and body to accomplish the impossible through my life." You are declaring that you cherish the presence of Jehovah God and that He is your provider, shield and ever-present help in times of trouble. You are acknowledging a simple trust in Him to be your all-in-all. Waiting on Him is saying "more of you Lord," while it open doors of favor and the supernatural to happen in your life.

The fascinating Old Testament tale about King Jehoshaphat's victory has always been a source of encouragement to my life. The fact is that if God did it for King Jehoshaphat, then he will do it now, because he is the same God yesterday, today and forever. He said to Malachi, *"I am the Lord and I do not change"* (Malachi 3:6). That same God is the God we serve today and what more! We are in the dispensation of grace, so I have no doubt in my heart that He is waiting with outstretched arms to cause the supernatural to happen in your life right now. For goodness sake, if

He did not spare His own son, but gave Him freely for us, how much more will He not also freely give us of all things requisite and suited to life and godliness?[15]

Reading about King Jehoshaphat has taught me about God's faithfulness in the times when challenges suddenly show up. Without a second thought, I have it impressed upon my heart that challenges are a stepping stone to a higher level of victory in the supernatural walk. Therefore, we must learn to walk and live above these trials. I have also learned about the pathway of praise that leads to supernatural provision and abundance of grace, which comes naturally for an heir of salvation.

One profound truth of this story that forever changed my life is that God always comes through for those who wait on Him. It doesn't matter how long it takes, God always shows up. The issue is not how big the problem is, but how great our God is, and whether we trust enough to wait on Him even in the presence of contrary evidence. All I know is that God comes through for those who wait on Him. Most importantly, He comes through in the most miraculous of ways.

Walking in the Supernatural

King Jehoshaphat[16] was busy leading God's people when the highest degree of opposition struck. Sometimes you are on your own, making sure to live right and stay within the boundary where God's love can reach you, when trouble suddenly strikes. Now, a multitude came against him in battle, and the king saw a threat to his government's stability. The peace of his nation was about to be destroyed in a battle that would most likely rend the kingdom from his hands. Bearing down upon him were unplanned chaos and catastrophe. Naturally, he was in fear and didn't know what to do. The soldiers who came against him were well-armed. Looking at the strength of his own forces, the king did not have all the resources needed to win the war. He did what he knew best, which is what children-of-God should do in these times, Jehoshaphat feared, "set himself to seek the Lord" and proclaimed a fast.

Jehoshaphat did more than just deliberate with his generals. He got out of his comfort zone and sought the Lord. He moved to wait on the Lord, so that he could renew his strength and sail to the other side of life's storms. He could do that because he trusted in the living God. He knew that no matter the situation, he had a God who could deliver him. What hit my spirit with excitement was that the king never looked at his problem's magnitude, but rather God's ability and power to deliver him. He took his eyes off the multitudes and fixed his eyes on the Lord. He stood in the assembly of Judah and Jerusalem in the house of the Lord before the nation and declared God's goodness. At that time, nothing about the situation was good, but God was and is always is good.

King Jehoshaphat handed everything to God and watched Him turn the situation around. When we allow God to take absolute control of our issues, he turns them around for His Glory. The multitudes that came against Jehoshaphat then turned against themselves and fought until they killed each other without leaving one survivor. What is also incredible is the amount of plunder that Jehoshaphat and his people found on the dead soldiers. That vast amount of treasures indicates God's favor upon Jehoshaphat and His people because they sought God. For any good to come out of your issues, God must be in absolute control of your life. Whenever you are faced with calamities, such as war, diseases or famine, you can stand in God's presence in humility, recognizing His sovereign authority. Honor his name and He will turn the darkest part of the night into dawn.

King Jehoshaphat and his people believed that God could deliver them from their enemies. They believed in His rescuing and that, no matter who came against them, God was able to give them victory even—as with the prophet Elijah's declaration to King Ahab—there was no sign in the cloud promising an abundance of rain. They sought the Lord, and waited on Him until they experienced victory. In troubled waters, I called on the Lord and He rescued me. Many times, I literally saw His hand move on my behalf. Sometimes, it did not look like He heard me, but I stayed with Him and reaped victory because I did not weaver in unbelief. The same will happen if you will only call upon Him because *"the Lord is near to those who call upon him."*[17] As you take out time to wait on the Lord concerning issues, you will see the supernatural happen in your life. He will give you answers and solutions you could have never imagined.

The enemy may have perverted the situation, but get a hold of God's eternal truth deep down in your spirit. You are created to rule and dominate in this life. Regardless of whether your future wife left you, bills are staring you in the face, or you get pregnant to a man who is not your husband, you must stay hooked to His presence. (My strong advice for unwed mothers-to-be is to keep the baby. Not aborting that baby may be the toughest decision you will ever have to make, but if you suffer for righteousness sake gains you integrity with God. He will go ahead of you and cause all the fragmented pieces of your life to fall in their proper place.)

Storms of life will come against you and, at times, you won't know what to do. You may be badly messed up from consequences of filth and sin, or with battles that threaten your peace. Your body may be inflicted with a dreadful disease and the doctors have written off your life. Some of your children may act like they are out of their minds, get strung out on drugs or end up incarcerated. When that happens, seek the Lord's face. While others are running wild on the streets, set yourself to seek God because He has already given you victory. You are victorious in Him and nothing can keep you down.

ENDNOTES

1. John 15:6
2. Hebrew 1:1,2 KJV (emphasis, added)
3. Genesis 26:13 KJV
4. Romans 8:1
5. Luke 5:1-8
6. Psalm 126:1
7. Romans 8:14
8. Hebrew 12:1 NLT
9. Galatians 5:19-21
10. Psalm 42:1
11. Psalm 119: 1
12. 1 Peter 2:9
13. Hebrew 4:16
14. Matthew 6:33 NLT
15. Romans 8:32 (emphasis, added)
16. 2 Chronicles 20:1-25 KJV
17. Psalms 145:18

Soul Search

1. What issues are you struggling with? (Make a list of the issues, but leave out the gory details because that could easily stir up lust in your heart)

2. What method(s) of approach do you intend to use in addressing these issues? (If you are in some danger of physical abuse, I advise that you prayerfully see a Christian counselor who will walk through the issues with you in wisdom)

3. How trusting are you in the power of God's mighty divine intervention in times of trouble? (Be as sincere as you can be in answering this question so that you can see for yourself where you need to make the changes about your perception in God's rescuing power.)

CHAPTER 3

What Do We Do While Waiting On the Lord?

PRAISE AND WORSHIP HIM CONTINUALLY

Make a joyful shout the Lord, all you lands! Serve the Lord with gladness; Come his presence with singing.[1]

The praise-worship pathway will take you into God's presence where you have the benefit of the fullness of His joy and pleasures forever more.[2] You must develop an attitude of praising and worshiping God as you wait on Him. Not only are we created for His pleasure, but this path leads to abundant life over issues that may have been written off for good. It is very easy to throw your hands up in the air and praise the Lord when all is going well. Most people praise the Lord because everything in their lives is working out right. Praise is good, and we are expected to praise God for all things.

While praise is good and indicative of our gratitude to God's provision and protection, there is a higher level and dimension, which is that intimate relationship where you get involved in with God. Worship is saying, "Okay, Lord. Have your way." When you worship Him, you are simply saying, "It is all about you Lord and nothing of me."

Worship is not about the material goods we receive from the Father: it has nothing to do with the car He gave, or the bills He paid. Provision is a direct reflection of what you get from "His hands," but something about seeking His "face" says "I want Lord." When you seek His face, you want Him for Him alone and not what he can give you. We worship Him because He is God all by himself. Worship says, "Lord, You are reigning and ruling in power and dominion." We worship Him because He is our sovereign God and absolute in our world. In worship, we can bow at His feet or fall flat at His face right in the middle of a crisis and say, "You are still on the throne Lord and nothing compares to you."

As we humbly bow down in praise-worship and adoration of His majesty, then He comes down to inhabit that praise-worship. Can you imagine what will happen when you live a life of praise-worship to God everyday? God will come down and inhabit those praises. For every praise-worship session you render to God, He steps into it to make a significant difference. When God steps down, what comes with Him is everything that makes Him God. He comes with healing, anointing, deliverance, protection, provision and so much more. No wonder He is called Jehovah El-shaddai, "the fully breasted one," and "God, who is more than enough." There is more than enough peace, joy, laughter, security, provision, healing, self-esteem and God esteem for those battered by and rejected in life.

Life-changing encounters occur in His presence as we break forth in praise-worship. When your world is falling apart, it may not sound logical to break out in praise-worship. Yes, it does not "sound" right, but it does get the job done. Praise-worship will move God on your behalf. Walls of containment will fall. That spirit of heaviness will lift off you and give way to righteousness, peace and joy in the Holy Ghost. Praise-worship always replaces despair. The beauty of His presence will replace the ashes that covered you, and the spirit of gladness will replace your days of mourning. As you continually move in the realm of knowing God with your praise-worship, supernatural doors of favor will be opened on your behalf.

Amidst trials and tribulation it's difficult to muster the ability to break forth in praise, worship and thanksgiving. But, take a look at how King Jehoshaphat gathered his people to praise the Lord when there was absolutely no reason to do so. In life, you must get beyond always having a reason to praise and worship God. Do it because He is God all by Himself and is worthy of our praise. Circumstances do not always have to be good before you can break out in praise-worship. The psalmist said, *"I will bless the Lord at all times; his praise shall continually be in my mouth."*[3]

Notice that praise is a matter of choice. No matter what you are going through, praising Him should be a choice-oriented and determined purpose. Yes, you do not feel like it, but praise is not about how you feel, it is about who He is. As you magnify God above everything else, what has tormented you will give way. Learn to magnify God at all times, for He is highly exalted and there is nothing He cannot do on the behalf of those who worship Him in truth and in the reality of His sovereign majesty. You serve a God with no limits to His reign, rule and sovereignty. That is why he is called the Most High God. You serve a praise-answering God. Make a decision today that you are going to wait on God with your praise and worship, then watch Him turn your life around.

King Jehoshaphat and His people had such confidence in God. They looked beyond their overwhelming situation, and praised and worshipped their way out. They were persuaded that God would come through for them. When you praise God, you are giving express approval of His sovereignty over your life. Praise-worship is that pathway to a deep, intimate relationship with him. When you reach this point in your walk, then He begins to reveal His ways to you. The more He reveals Himself to you, the better you get at admiring and magnifying Him, standing in awe of Him, lifting Him high above everything and acknowledging His Lordship and supremacy over your life.

When you are hard-pressed on all sides, you must look beyond your situation and your circumstance to praise God. At the very moment King Jehoshaphat and his people began to sing and give praise to God, He caused the multitude that came against them to start fighting among themselves. Do you know that God is also able to turn-around your situation for good? Begin to look at what He can do with His mighty hands because the "issue" that confronts you is not the problem. What is truly important is whether you believe that God is able to come through for you. For more on the subject of praise and worship, please refer to a life-changing book I read numerous times: *The Purpose and Power of Praise and Worship* by Dr. Myles Munroe.[4]

Effect of Praise-Worship

Praise-worship will shut down the enemy's voice and cause him to flee in many directions because God will have picked-up the fight on your behalf. To fight spiritual warfare with carnal weapons makes no sense, for you will always be defeated. When pressures come against you, anchor on the Lord because He has given you the victory over all the enemy's wiles. God has fought every single battle you would have had to fight in your life. The blood-stained banner of our Lord Jesus Christ is there to remind you to walk in victory every single day. When King Jehoshaphat and his army arrived at the war site, dead bodies were scattered all over the ground and not one single adversary had escaped. When the king sought the Lord in praise and worship, he discovered the key to walking in the supernatural.

When King Jehoshaphat and his men gathered the plunder, they found vast amount of equipment, clothing and other valuables. There was so much plunder that it took them three days to collect it all. I never understood the reason why these armies fought with valuables on them, except for the fact that God positions us for a miraculous, supernatural shift in our level of prosperity when we stay focused on Him. King Jehoshaphat would never have reaped this supernatural shift in his level of prosperity, if had he had not sought God's face and praised his way through the multitude. The victory turned out to be beyond their wildest imagination. They became rich because they sought the face of God and, beyond that, came the experience of peace, joy and victory.

The Key to Unlocking Impossible Doors

Alongside praise and worship, there is one other key that unlocks impossible doors. Many people do not realize this, but prayer is one key you cannot afford to be without. While waiting on the Lord, you must commit yourself to a life of prayer. Prayer is a broad subject, but for the purpose of this assignment, I will approach it from specific angles. Prayer is a fellowship in reverential awe with the Father. It is seeking His face and communing with Him, and it is also the place of making our supplications known to Him in the name of Jesus Christ. Prayer is talking to the Father and it is the contact point at which He hears us. Knowing that He hears us at the place of prayer, we ought always to acknowledge His sovereign power in our lives.

Simply put, prayer is that intimate place of connecting with Him. When your innermost desires yearn for Him in prayer with an indescribable passion, you will experience a touch of God upon your life incomprehensible to the finite mind. Prayer activates an anointing around you so heavy that it stops satan right in his tracks. Many Christians do not spend time in prayer and, due to its absence, their lives are marked by an unimaginably high failure rate. They are too busy with the affairs of this world to spend quality time with the Father in prayer. God is waiting for you to come into communion with Him. He longs to fellowship with you, but you can never truly know Him and the power of His resurrection if you do not spend time in prayer.

The book of Jeremiah tells us, *"that he watches over his word to perform it"* (Jeremiah 1:12). God does want to perform all those things He has said concerning you. But this can only happen when you come to Him in prayer to unlock those hidden treasures. Praying to the Father indicates that you know all power belongs to Him. All our combined natural strengths and abilities are limited without Him. We become strengthened and perfected when we stay in communion with Him. You can never remain the same when you spend time in prayer because it releases tremendous power for you to walk over situations. You have no control over life without Him and, therefore, need constant fellowship with our supreme God. He is the entire source of our existence. You cannot please Him if you do not believe that He will reward your sincerity in seeking hard after Him.

I urge you to spend time in prayer and watch how God moves on the behalf of those who wait on Him in prayer. When you are connected to God, His abundant mercy, grace and love will begin to cascade upon you like the dew of Hermon. I am not so concerned about that dead situation staring you in the face. But I am concerned that you activate God's power in prayer so His mighty hand will move on your behalf to level every mountain and fill up every valley in your life. Because we go to prayer for hearing and answering God, I have no doubt that if you seek Him sincerely, He will move on your behalf. Even if He does not deliver you from the troubles, I know that He will surely deliver you through them.

The Lord will answer your prayers according to His will for your life and not according to your own will. The will of God for your life is His word. It is written, *"For all the promises of God in him are yes and in him Amen,"*[5] meaning that whatever you lift up to Him in prayer is already settled. The Word of God is absolute in your world of containment. He wants to break open those barriers and set you free. He has plans stored in the Word for you, and those plans are for today and the future, and for good and not evil. He purposes to make you soar like an eagle in a down world.

Jesus Christ taught the disciples to pray, *"Your kingdom come. Your will be done on earth as it is in heaven."*[6] Here, He was referring to the Father's will, which are those words He has spoken about you in the Scriptures. This equation clearly shows you that prayer cannot be separated from the Word of God. You have to know what He says concerning every situation in your life and then present your case to Him by faith in the name of Jesus Christ. Because we trust God, we should not be afraid to pray for the Father's will to be done in our lives, regardless of what we believe the end result should be.

Knowing that he predestined us even before the beginning of the world, our future is secure with Him. He is the Alpha and the Omega, the Beginning and the End of all things: you never need to be afraid to trust Him. He knows everything that concerns us. His word is sure, and it is forever settled in Heaven. The Word will never go back to Him empty, but must accomplish that which it was sent to do. When you seek the Lord in prayer, you are saying to Him *"Not my will Lord, but your will be done in my life God"* (Matthew 26:39) and, according to the Bible, He will direct your path when you trust Him.[7] Direction comes when we wait on the Lord in prayer. With the Lord in direction, you can be sure that no demon in hell can stop His agenda for your life. Because you sought His face in prayer, He will bring your plans to an expected end. Always remember that God is good and He is interested in all that concerns you.

Knowing the Will of God Through Prayer

When you spend time in His presence, you learn what pleases Him. Because the will of God for your life is His word, you know that you are on course when everything lines up the Word laid up in your heart. The Word of God will bring life to your circumstances and that is why God admonishes us *"not to forget the Law but to keep his commands in our heart."*[8] Knowing God's will is experiencing a tranquility that surpasses natural understanding because the *rhema* word bears witness in our spirit. *Rhema*, or words of divine revelation, comes through continuous fellowship with Him in prayer. When we are connected, the Holy Ghost exposes spiritual truths to us. When you lift up a situation before God in prayer, you become aware of His will for you through the Word-based peace you experience in the situation. When life has hit you with a bad deal and there is absolutely no need to laugh, you will be able to laugh because His peace negates human reasoning.

When you violate the will of God by disobeying His word, the peace you once experienced steps aside. What you are left with is the conflict of inner turmoil. You must guard your heart with all caution because life-giving issues flow from within you. The devil is not after what you possess. Believe me, he can't drive your cars, wear your clothes or spend your money. Satan is after deeper issues, like the peace of God that guards your heart. Once the devil succeeds in disarming peace from your heart, he can come in and mess up your life majestically. When you are not experiencing the peace of God, satan can do anything he wants. Guard your heart and align your priorities with God's will by praying in accordance with the word. That is the best way of shutting all doors on the enemy.

Benefits of Using the Key

When you live a life of prayer and consecration, God's anointing will come upon your life in a special way and you will begin to walk in power. Because you dared to believe in Him and stayed faithful in prayer, signs and wonders will follow. This miraculous power will draw men unto God. You will cast out demons in His name, speak with new tongues, take up serpents and if you drink anything deadly, it will certainly not harm you. You will also see the sick healed as you lay hands on them.[9] Signs and wonders will be evident through you because His anointing rubs off on those who spend much time in prayer. In prayer, you build up yourself in a most holy faith[10] and the Lord will work mightily through you. Look at the life of Jesus Christ: He was a man of prayer and God wrought miracles through Him.

> *Afterward he went up into the hill by himself to pray. Night fell while he was there alone.*[11]

> *Then an angel appeared from heaven and strengthened him. He prayed more fervently and he was in such agony of spirit that his sweat fell to the ground like great drops of blood.*[12]

Because Jesus spent quality time alone with the Father, He was strengthened and was always in control of what happened around Him. Many signs and wonders accompanied his ministry and the source of that power was time in prayer with the Father. I declare boldly that nothing can take the place of prayer in your life. Defining moments are changed in prayer. Life becomes meaningful when you pray. Destinies are changed and dead issues brought back to life. Dead marriages have been resurrected because some wife dared to pray. Street kids strung out on drugs picked up the pieces of their lives because some grandmother dared to pray. Some wife-battering, adulterous husband came home and turned his slapping hands into faithful comforting ones, all because a mother dared to pray. God turned my life around because I prayed. What would he not do for you if you will only pray? I encourage you today to begin spending time with God in prayer and see what He will do in your life. Cultivate a relationship with Jesus that will enable Him to demonstrate His power through you and give you control over situations and circumstances.

> *A final word, be strong in the Lord's mighty power. Put on all of God's armor so that you will be able to stand firm against all strategies and tricks of the devil. For we are not fighting against people made of flesh and blood but against the evil rulers and authorities of the unseen world, against those mighty powers of darkness who rule this world, and against wicked spirits in the heavenly realms.*[13]

If the eyes of our spirit were opened to the spirit realm, we would quickly get up from our comfort zones to prohibit the devil's works in fervent prayer. A lot of evil exists out in the world, but, as children of the Most High God, we have been given power to subdue schemes of the evil one. If you don't know the depth of your spiritual authority, you will constantly live in defeat. We are a waging a spiritual warfare that does not go up against flesh-and-blood. Until we move in the spirit realm clad in God's battle armor, we will continue to engage in the mediocre lifestyle of our failed, defeated past. Abundant life will elude us because we lack of knowledge in the Lord.

We have power given to us from on high to decide what we want to happen to us. What you allow to happen is in your hands: whatsoever we bind on earth will be bound and what ever we loose will be loosed.[14] Our Lord Jesus Christ spoke definite and absolute words: when he said "whatsoever," He meant whatsoever. Put on God's armor and move into the battlefield to prohibit demonic works from gaining a foothold in your life. The victory has already been won when Jesus died in your place. As you daily strengthen yourself under the Lord's mighty power, you will be able to stand firm against the devil's stratagems.

Hindrances to Effective Use of the Key

Consciously or otherwise, we sometimes engage in activities that rob us of our God-given dreams. These missteps prevent us from reaching heights we ought to be attaining in realms of supernatural elevation. God's desire is for us to walk in depths of power that come as a result of time spent in prayer with Him. Let us look at a series of serious hindrances.

Missing the Mark

Acts of sin will cause you to fall out of fellowship with God. A mark set before us and when we miss that mark due to a weight of sin, we end up missing Him. Once you are out of fellowship with God, you cannot behold the beauty of His presence. Take a critical look at what happened to Adam and Eve in the Garden of Eden: they fell out of fellowship with God by falling short of the perfect standard set for them by God. They turned their back on Him and, consequently, lost out on the divine position of their birthright. They could no longer go into God's presence as before, so they went into hiding naked and ashamed. *"Towards evening they heard the Lord God walking about in the garden, so they hid themselves among the trees. The Lord God called to Adam, "where are you?" He replied, "I heard you, so I hid. I was afraid because I was naked."*[15] When you miss the mark of God's calling on your life, you get disconnected from His presence. Your divine shelter caves in and then, all of a sudden, your life is naked and you are ashamed.

When sin strips your spiritual covering, it will cost you dignity, confidence, boldness and peace. The action that breaks God's laws and commandments is that very same action breaks your fellowship with God. When you cannot get into His presence and have fellowship, how can you expect to have communion with God so your prayers are answered? Fellowship with God is very important in order to stay in His presence. If you maintain a regular relationship with God through prayer, you are less likely to yield to temptations of sin in your life. As you continually maintain fellowship with God, you will enjoy the purity that comes from abiding in His presence. This is not to say that you will not face temptations that arise from daily life. How strong you are on the inside is what will keep you righteous when all else points to the direction of compromise.

Beloved, I pray that you may prosper and be in good health just as your soul prospers.[16]

The sustaining factor through life's turbulence is what's inside you, because the ability to resist temptation comes from inner strength. What are you doing with the Holy Ghost inside you? Have you allowed Him to be your wonderful counselor or is your mind taking you where you want to go? There is absolutely no way you can ever say "no" to sin if you are weak inside. You will not divinely prosper on the outside, if you are spiritually improvised within. What you do to your spirit man is so crucially important.

A couple of years ago, I visited a construction site where Frank and his civil engineering team were building the foundation to erect a communications tower. I noticed that they excavated the pit for the foundation and filled it with lots of cement re-enforcement rods and chips. After that, they covered the surface with concrete and cement. The next time I visited the construction site, I noticed the tower standing tall on its foundation. You will never guess how deep and solidly built that foundation was. As children of God, our foundation must be saturated deep down with Scripture because God's word is what will keep you from falling. When the Word dwells richly within, you will have the stability to face what comes against you.

You have to be solid-as-rock inside and filled with the knowledge of His will. You must be filled with power and anointing, and be rooted and grounded in Him and His word. There are grades and standards in our walking relationship with the Lord. Your highest standard is that you are solidly built with a firm foundation in the Word of God. You ought to have depth in your relationship with Him as He unveils Himself to you daily. Then, when the pressures of life arise, you will be found standing firm. You will not be swayed by sin because, on the inside, you are so prosperous with His word that it flows on your outside.

UNFORGIVENESS!

Unforgiveness is a thick hindrance to prayer: it robs you of a sweet relationship with God, and stands as a stumbling block in our love relationship with the Father. Unforgiveness is a root cause of bitterness, and, once it has found place in your spirit, you can never give birth to the promises of God for your life. Unforgiveness has a track record of blocking all God's intents for His children. God does not want us to walk in unforgiveness. But bitterness towards those who have hurt us is what allows us to remain unforgiving. We are angry about what does not work in our lives, and we are so sore with past guilt that it bound to the point of refusing to forgive ourselves.

But if you refuse to forgive others, your heavenly Father will not forgive you.[17]

Lack of forgiveness on your part will cause the root of bitterness to spring up from within. Because God is Holy, he cannot behold your bitterness. No person and no situation is worth paying such a price for. If you are not walking in the forgiveness of God, then you cannot experience His abundant life. In order to experience this life, you need to release those who have hurt you. Forgive yourself, let go of the guilt and enjoy God. Unforgiveness is a fleshly desire, and the desires of the flesh always war against the desires of the spirit. If you yield to any fleshly desire, you will break the Holy Spirit's flow in your life. Where you could otherwise flow naturally into God's presence, you will feel a brick wall between you and Him when you pray because unforgiveness blocks the flow of communication. Much more than that, unforgiveness takes away our peace. If you refuse to forgive, your life will be one of constant conflict.

The Overconfidence of Self-Exaltation

Many people have to deal with pride every day. Some realize it, while others do not. Pride, which is the overconfidence of self-exaltation, has a subtle way of rearing its head when we choose to walk according to our ways. We do so out of a false belief that we are equal to the task. We want to be our own boss because we can't imagine submitting to anyone else. Why create an exaggerated opinion of yourself when the Word of God defines who you are? Pride is an understated treachery. You can easily find yourself out of God's move if you are not careful to validate your inner desires as truly turned towards God. Look at what happened to Lucifer, who had everything going for him: loved by God, he was the center of show, and enjoyed His presence until his desired to take God's place. Lucifer's desires were so skewed that wanted God's position instead of His presence.

> *How are you fallen from heaven, O shining star, son of the morning! You have been thrown down to the earth, you who destroyed the nations of the world. For you said to yourself, "I will ascend and set my throne above God's stars. I will preside on the mountains of the*

gods far away from the north. I will climb to the highest heavens and be like the Most High." But instead, you will be brought down to the place of the dead, down to its lowest depths.[18]

A will and desire to exalt yourself is what will take you out of the presence of God. The root cause of pride lurks deep down in the hearts of those not totally humble before God. Sometimes, we are ignorant of pride, but it is the one quality that God Almighty resists, yet He does give grace to the humble. All Lucifer sought was to ascend and be like the Most High God. He was not content with the position given him by God. Watch out for discontentment, which is usually a set up for failure to disconnect you from your Source of life. God knows the need in your life. When you humble yourself under the mighty hand of God, he will lift you up. Lucifer was no longer content with His relationship with God. What disloyalty! Any time we seek God with an egocentric motive, we mock Him. The truth of the matter is that our egocentricity will take us out of His presence because God cannot be mocked. Remember that, *"whatever a man sows, that shall he reap"* (Galatians 6:7).

God was not impressed with Lucifer's self-centered desire to take on God's position, and that arrogance lost Lucifer his fellowship with God. Once that happened, Lucifer also lost the presence. Lucifer had the will to go further than the ability of the Most High God. He committed high treason and, fast as a flash-of-lightning, God cast Lucifer out of heaven. It is important to allow God search and expose any will in your life that is misaligned with the Father's will. God does not advance the agenda of those who seek to exalt themselves, because every position of influence comes from Him.

Anytime you get into the move of God and run after Him with a hidden agenda, you nullify the effect of God's grace in your life. You can never find fulfillment in life when you go after God for the wrong reasons.

Scripture confirms that when it says, *"but those who exalt themselves will be humbled, and those who humble themselves will be exalted."*[19] You can never get far with God when you are proud about the dealings and affairs of life. If you humble yourself under is mighty arms, He will exalt you in His time because that is when He makes things beautiful. Humility is not a feeling, but rather a submission of your will to the Lord: it is a specific, definite, modest and un-exaggerated opinion of your own importance.

We Ask Amiss

Finally, our prayers are hindered because we ask amiss, which means making requests selfishly so as to spend on our wild passions. One fundamental cause of asking amiss is greed. We want what we crave and, after we get it, we are still not content. Our watchword becomes "more, more, more." Typical of a greed that is never full, the quest in life for many is "more." Our prayers will always be hindered when our gratification is only for personal desires and not for that which moves eternity.

> *You ask and do not receive, because you ask amiss, that you may spend it on your pleasure.*[20]

When we ask with wrong motives, we do not receive because we only wish to satisfy our untamed passions. What are your motives when you come to God in prayer? Where is your will in the move of God in your life? If you are sincere with yourself, you will understand why you are where you are today. If you are never really making any progress in your prayer life, check your motives. Are you consumed with your passions to "have," and so inundated by your desires faced when not received from God? God's desire is for us to have everything that pertain to life and godliness, but your priorities must be aligned with His will for your life. When we forget about our selfishness to pursue hard after Him, and seek

Him first above all we desire, then He will cause all things to abound in our favor. Believe me when I say, "all things will literally chase you."

Fasting That Pleases God

Fasting is a period of time of going without food for the purpose of seeking God's face. Great things happen when you fast in combination with prayer and studying Scripture. You become a more disciplined person and your innermost desires are humbled. Without the distraction of what gratifies the flesh, you give yourself over more to prayer. This enables your body's appetites to be crucified. How you go about fasting—to discipline yourself, break strongholds, build up your confidence in God and bring to subjection your innermost desires—all depends on you. Fasting does not have any closely controlled rules-and-regulations. Aside from abstaining from food, you can choose to abstain from whatever else distracts you from seeking Him. When it regards abstinence, it is your faith in God that is being built up. If you only knew what your untamed desires have truly caused, you would give yourself over to fasting to discipline your appetites and gain ascendancy over that controls. All said and done, I want to lay emphasis on what God calls a true fast.

> *No, the kind of fasting I want calls you to free those who are wrongly imprisoned and to stop oppressing those who work for you. Treat them fairly and give them what they earn. I want you to share your food with the hungry and to welcome poor wanderers into your homes. Give clothes to those who need them, and do not hide from relatives who need your help. If you do these things, your salvation will come like the dawn. Yes, your healing will come quickly. Your godliness will lead you forward, and the glory of the lord will lead you forward, and the glory of the Lord will protect you from behind. Then when you call, the Lord will answer. "Yes, I*

am here,: he will quickly reply. "Stop oppressing the helpless and stop making false accusations and spreading vicious rumors! Feed the hungry and help those in trouble. Then your light will shine out from the darkness, and the darkness around you will be bright as day. The Lord will guide you continually, watering your life when you are dry and keeping you healthy, too. You will be like a well-watered garden, like an ever-flowing spring. [21]

Has anyone wrongly imprisoned you with his thoughts, words, or action? You will need to let go whatever judgments you have passed against them. That burden is too heavy to carry. You are desperate for a touch from On High, yet you strongly hold onto to that which does not count towards eternity. You need to see yourself soaring high and this happens when you "let go and let God." Holding on that you ought to let go of is an expensive game that you cannot afford to play. What is your attitude towards those who work for you? Do you give them what rightfully belongs to them or do your treat them as if they don't matter in life's equation. God is looking at the intents of your heart. What do you do when meeting those disadvantaged people who are unaware that they can have more from God? The eyes of the Lord are truly going through out this earth, and He is going to bless that person whose heart is matured towards Him.

In all of this, God wants us to keep His statues and commands. When we do so, He will guide us continually. All dry areas of our lives will be watered, and there is a divine promise to keep us healthy. This is the fast that the Lord has chosen. Add value to people's lives, make it easy for those around you to enjoy life, and share your food with the hungry and cloth the naked. God cannot lie and cannot be mocked; He will do what He says. He has promised that your own light will break forth when you undo burdens, free the oppressed and share with the needy. Your healing will spring up speedily and your righteousness shall go before you. The

Lord shall be your rear-guard. Such a fast is God-focused and not man-focused. As you wait on the Lord and increase the fruit of your righteousness, your healing will spring forth speedily.

Renewing Your Mind with the Word

Nothing good can ever come out of a mind not recreated by the Spirit of the God. When you accept Jesus Christ into your life, realize that your spirit—the real you—gets born with the spirit of God. This fusion automatically makes your spirit alive; you have received eternal life when your spirit is born-again with the Spirit of God. You now have the God-kind of life, which is eternal life. The very essence of God, the spirit of life, comes to live inside you.[22] But your emotional and mental power, which make up your very essence, are not automatically saved when you accept Christ.

You have spent an entire life feeding your mind with what does not count towards eternity, which is everything about the world's system of operation. Now you need to allow the Word of God renew your mind and cleanse it from all the filth the world system has dropped in your soul. *"Don't copy the behavior and customs of the world, but let God transform you into a new person by changing the way you think. Then you will know what God wants you to do, and you will know how good and pleasing and perfect his will really is."*[23] You will have to do away with everything that is not in line with God's agenda for your life. For that very reason, you must spend serious time putting the Word of God into your heart through your ears, eyes and mouth. Knowing how God wants you to live this life is a very important issue that you cannot afford to take for granted. Only the Word of God can change you; you cannot change yourself. If you do not have His word stored in your heart, then you cannot be what God has called you to be. You need to accept the Word of God into your heart so that you are saved from destruction.[24]

The natural man, who is the unsaved man, is made of a spirit, has a soul and lives in a body. Due to sin and iniquity, his spirit is dead and completely separated from God. But his body is alive and touches and makes contact with the world. His essence, inner being and wishes are filled with everything that comes through the body. What comes through contact with the world are the yearning of the eyes and flesh for life's pleasures. When the natural man gets born again, his spirit becomes dead to sin, flesh and all its pleasures. The spirit in him is now made alive because God's spirit now indwells him. You are only made alive in the spirit when you crucify the flesh. Because flesh will always fight spirit, the process to crucify flesh will be a daily affair. All that your soul knows is what has been fed to it through the body.

As a born-again, spirit-filled child of God, you should think the way God wants you to. Your mind is where your passion and mental power reside. As an unbeliever you thought according to the world system, so now you will have to renew your mind with the Word of God. As your mind is being transformed daily with His word, your body gets set free from sin because His word, and not your body, determines how you live. When your spirit is alive, you will begin to experience life abundantly. When the Spirit of God is in operation in your life, all your displeasures, peevishness, frustrations and fleshly desires that once controlled you now give way to the Spirit of God. His spirit keeps sending you restoration from dead works and carnal desires.

Your mind receives these messages of restoration and sends them to your body, which gets free from transgression and ruin. Now the Word you can use in any situation is what seals your mind. The Word of God in your spirit will work through your mind and get the job done in your body. Most believers have a problem with the conflict that rages inside them. This conflict is termed carnality. The carnal man's spirit, soul, and body are alive because he has asked Jesus to come into his heart, but his mind is trapped in a battle between the control of flesh and spirit. He does want to live right, but he is stuck. What he does not want to do is actually what he ends up doing. If your mind is not renewed with the Word of God, then you will do whatever your mind tells you to do. But if you store up God's word within you, that word will expose what is unlike God, so you can deal with it and move on.

You need the Word of God on a consistent basis to get past your mind, so that you are not swinging up-and-down the ladder of development in the Lord. Having the Word of God down in your spirit will transform your life. Whatever the problem is, meditating on the Word of God will cause that situation to turn around for your benefit. That is why you cannot play with the Word of God and have it absent from your life.

> *For the word that God speaks is alive and full of power [making it active, operative, energizing and effective]; it is sharper than any two-edged sword, penetrating to the dividing line of the breath of life (soul) and [immortal] spirit, and joints and marrow [of the deepest parts of nature], exposing and sifting and analyzing and judging the very thoughts and purposes of the heart.* [25]

The Word that God speaks has the living power to work positively in the direction of your life and take its place in your spirit and your issues. The word will quicken whatever deadness is around you. Because of its quickening and dynamic supremacy, only God's word can bring the revelation. At one time in my life, I struggled with bitterness and unforgiveness for so long that I lost my peace, felt very discomforted and was empty. So many other aspects of my life were dysfunctional because the Most High was not in charge. The power of God was not activated upon my life. I felt that my life was simply falling apart. I closed in and became very withdrawn, but the Holy Spirit started to deal with me on certain issues. I knew the time had come to take those untamed works of the flesh into the Holy Spirit's presence to be dealt with.

Some of you reading these words cannot relate to what I am saying because your emotions are locked-up to the point where you have become cold and indifferent. Absolutely nothing stirs up any type of feeling within you. If you are tired of being cold, indifferent and disconnected from life, this is for you. You are saved and filled with the Holy Ghost, but you are up against the flesh, which must be crucified daily until the Holy Spirit helps you gain mastery and control of our emotions. Had it not been for the Lord who is on our side, many of us would have gone down the lane of statistics due to the tragic results of untamed emotions.

I studied Scripture that helped me deal with my emotions. Some people act like they have no emotions at all, but some of us are glad that there's a High Priest who is touched with the feelings of our infirmities; when we are weak, His strength is made perfect in our weakness. As I continued to meditate on His word, I one day realized that all my bitterness and anger had gone. I recognized that what was happening to me was a set up: the devil was after my peace because it is the peace of God that guards my heart. So waiting in the presence of God—and speaking the Word over the bitterness and disconnection from life—got me to the point where my emotions were under the Holy Spirit's control. When we come to His saving power, we are the ones who will make our ways prosperous by meditating upon the Word.[26] Stay on the Word until you see that light arising in that tunnel of discontentment and make your way prosperous.

Living a Spirit-Filled Life

So I advise you to live according to your new life in the Holy Spirit when you won't be doing what your sinful nature craves. The old sinful nature loves to do evil, which is just opposite from what the Holy Spirit wants and the Spirit gives us desires opposite from what the sinful nature desires. These two forces are constantly fighting each other and your choices are never free from their conflict. When you are directed by the Holy Spirit, you are no longer under the desires of your sinful nature and your lives will produce these evil results: sexual immorality, impure thoughts, eagerness for lustful pleasures, idolatry, participation in demonic activities hostility, quarrelling, jealousy, outburst of anger, selfish ambition, divisions, the feeling that everyone is wrong except those in your own little group, envy, drunkenness, wild parties and other kinds of sin. Let me tell you again, as I have before, that anyone living that sort of life will not inherit the kingdom of God.[27]

If the Holy Spirit is not leading you, you are obviously headed in the wrong direction, because you are leading yourself and, believe me, you do not know the way. The Holy Spirit's leading is absolutely necessary because your fleshy desires are in competition with what the Holy Spirit wants to accomplish through your life. That is the reason why your emotions must be tamed and controlled by the Holy Ghost. Many times we live in deception because our motives for coming to God are for self-centered ambitions. Are you only after what you want or do you desire what the Spirit of God wants to deposit in you? If you live and walk in the Spirit always, you will not gratify fleshly desires. If our lives are controlled by our passions and desires, there is no way we can be what God has called us to be.

Living a Spirit-filled life means that you allow Him to constantly have supremacy over your life, as you behold Him in the beauty of His holiness. In essence, that lifestyle means walking in the Word of God. The flesh is crucified by bringing the lust of the flesh, the lust of the eyes and the pride of life into captivity to the obedience of our Lord

Jesus Christ. As you submit yourself to God's leading through His word and anointing, the desire to do what you want fades. When you devote your time to the Holy Spirit, you will know more of Christ and become more like Him. Consequently, you will only seek to do that which pleases God. Experiencing a Spirit-filled life stems from a relationship with God where all your passions, cravings, wants and needs are completely taken over by Him.

I liken the Holy Spirit infilling to a pitcher being filled with orange juice until it starts to overflow. Now the measure of the juice is the level of the juice inside the pitcher. Once the pitcher it is full, no space remains to contain the juice, and what overflows is the same juice that filled up the pitcher in first place. The same goes for the measure of the Holy Ghost within you. To the degree you let Him pour into you, that is the degree that He fills. The more you decrease is the more He increases in you. You need to get to that point in your relationship with God where you have the Holy Ghost to the point of overflow. You have so decreased that He just keeps filling you up. Suddenly your life is filled to the brim with Him and you begin to overflow with the fruits of love, joy, peace, patience, gentleness, kindness and self-control.[28]

From the character of one under His control, the Holy Spirit removes qualities that are not true, pure, humble, and worthy of honor and good report, worthy of honor, and replaces it fills with His abiding presence. My desire is that you will live a life led by the Spirit of the living God. That way, you will do what is right freely, and not by compulsion of the Law. Living a life not controlled by the Holy Spirit can be very frustrating: you want to do right but your carnal nature constantly competes with your Spirit. As such, you are always in conflict with yourself, which is not a happy way to live. But as you submit to Him daily, He builds character and values in you.

FELLOWSHIP AND SERVICE IN THE COURTS

It is so important that we serve in the courts of our Lord and fellowship with other believers. But, many of us only have fellowship with our jobs and all manners of wrong relationships. We never make it to the house of God because we are busy trying to fix our lives in a way that only God can. King David got to a point in his life where he said to himself, *"...I would rather be a doorkeeper in the house of my God than dwell in the tents of wickedness."*[29] He found out that all we seek with such tenacity amounts to nothing if God is not the focal point. King David knew the importance of being in God's house, having fellowship with other believers and rendering service to Him because those planted in His house are the ones that flourish.

You cannot be waiting on the Lord and be hanging around the devil's joints. Today, many Christians are out there just doing you're their thing. They claim that they know God; their lives have all the forms of godliness, but deny the power of God therein. You have to be, as the cliché goes, in the right place at the right time, because you need God's covering upon your life. You cannot make it alone. Being a part of the body of Christ is vitally important in the race of this life. When you are in the wrong place at the right time, the enemy can have his time in your life. This happens because when satan came to you, he could identify a lot of himself within your life. To mix with people who have no relationship with God and still expect to keep God-given values is a deception straight from the pit of hell.

> *Oh the joys of those who do not follow the advice of the wicked, or stand around with sinners, or join in with scoffers. But they delight in doing every thing the Lord wants day and night, they think about his law. They are like trees planted along the riverbank, bearing*

fruit each season without fall. Their leaves never wither, and in all they do, they prosper.[30]

Where you will hear much about the law of the Lord, if you do not make His house your primary focus. There is no reason to form strong, bonding relationships with unbelievers because it will dent your God-given principles, loyalty, integrity and steadfastness. This does not mean to go so far as to isolate yourself from unbelievers either, because you "have been commissioned to go out and make disciples of all Nations." You will meet non-believers just about everywhere you go. You are expected to take the Gospel of Jesus to the world, but do whatever you ought to stay focused by the Holy Spirit's help. Define your different types of relationships, and then stay loyal to the One who called you out of darkness into His marvelous light. When you focus on Him, instead of all manner of relationships, you will not lose sight of your destination. People around you may feed their minds with all sorts of junk; but you cannot afford to, if you want to remain concerned about your values, character and relationship with God.

Can there be any relationship between the temple of God and idols? If you have truly discovered God, you cannot afford to live a life of compromise. You can't afford to be unequally yoked in wrong relationships, because these wrong relationships will hurt you. You will lose grip of yourself and your eternal relationship with God. The issue here is not so much the unbelieving people around you, as much as it is your will to remain focused, stay strong and do the right thing. If you lack a solid foundation in the Lord, hanging out with people who do not share your values is not wise. What you need is the Word of God, because the devil already has his eyes on you when you mix anointing. What you ought to do is developing your strength of character with the Word of God.

Again, this does not mean to isolate yourself from the unbelievers around you. They will be in the offices where you work, in the malls, on the streets, in the parking lot, in the parks and everywhere else. In the Great Commission, our Lord Jesus Christ instructed us go into the world and preach the Gospel so that men might be saved. You are the one who has message of redemption for the world out there. The message they have is one of destruction. What I consider priority in divine walk is that we do not compromise our God-given standards. Unbelievers have all sorts of wrong values which will rub off on you, if do not maintain your position in the Lord. No matter how hard you try to play it safe, getting involved in an intimate relationship with them on a consistent basis will shift your values, commitment and standards.

Playing in the enemy's camp will cost you a chosen walk with God. I am well aware that there is no way to totally separate yourself from every surrounding influence, but you do have the power and innate ability to resist that which is not of God. Like the saying goes, "You may not be able to stop a bird from flying over your head, but you certainly can stop it from building its nest on your head." The people you want to constantly fellowship with is your choice to make. You can never stop people from speaking to you, but you can decide whom you listen to. Ours is a world of corruption and the only way to stay above compromise is by dwelling in the "secret place."

It will not be in your interest to forsake the assembly of believers. The enemy is out to get you when your feet are not planted in God's house. Once he can get you by yourself, it will be easy for him to get you to fall. Fellowshipping with other believers will help sharpen your life, and create an avenue for you to grow spiritually and be involved in something larger than "yourself." When life's challenges hit you, there are good people around to hold your hands in prayer and intercede along with you. Apart from building up your life, commitment and integrity, there are blessings that come from fellowshipping in the house of the Lord. When we fellowship with one another we build unity, and the Lord commands His blessings on unity. If you want to have a touch of God's blessings upon your life, stay in fellowship with the brethren.[31] If you desire a touch from God, and want His blessings and life poured out on your issues, then do not forsake the assemblies of believers.

ENDNOTES

1. Psalm 100:1
2. Psalm 16:11 (emphasis added)
3. Psalm 34: 1
4. Dr. Myles Munroe: *The Purpose and Power of Praise and Worship* (Copyright 2000- Myles Munroe, Destiny Image Publishers, Inc. P.O. Box 310, Shippensburg, PA 17257-0310 USA, In partnership with The Diplomat Center Carmichael Road, P. O. Box N- 9583 Nassau Bahamas)
5. 2 Corinthians 1:20
6. Matthew 6:10
7. Proverbs 3:5-6
8. Proverbs 3:1 (emphasis added)
9. Mark 16:17-18
10. Jude 1:20
11. Matthew 14:23 NLT
12. Luke 22:43-44 NLT
13. Ephesians 6:10-12 NLT
14. Matthew 18:18
15. Genesis 3:8-10 NLT
16. 3 John 2
17. Matthew 6:15 NLT
18. Isaiah 14:12-15 NLT

19. Matthew 23:12 NLT
20. James 4:3
21. Isaiah 58: 6-11 NLT
22. 1 John 5:11-12
23. Romans 12:2 NLT
24. James 1:21
25. Hebrew 4:12 AMP
26. Joshua 1:8
27. Galatians 5:16-21 NLT
28. Galatians 5:22
29. Psalm 84:10
30. Psalm 1:1-3 NLT
31. Psalm 133:1-3

Soul Search

1. How has praise-worship, prayer, fasting, and fellowship affected you lately?

2. What are your motives all about when you come before God in prayer?

3. How united is your life with the Father's will?

4. What God-given values do you have in common with your friends?

CHAPTER 4

If You Don't Give Up, You Won't Cave In

God will bring you out of any messy situation if only you make a divine connection with Him. Once you make that connection in His presence, those circumstances will dry up and give way for wholeness to be poured into you. Let us go through the life experience of the woman with the issue-of-blood[1] and see how a divine connection with the Lord Jesus Christ supernaturally transformed her life. Not only was she transformed, but Jesus put all the broken, disoriented and fragmented parts of her life back together.

Now a certain woman had a flow of blood for 12 years, and had suffered many things from many physicians. She had spent all that she had, yet only grew worse.

When she heard about Jesus, she came behind Him in the crowd and touched His garment. For she said, "If only I may touch His

> *clothes, I shall be made well." Immediately the fountain of her blood was dried up and she felt in her body that she was healed of the affliction. And Jesus, immediately knowing that power had gone out of Him, turned around in the crowd and said, "Who touched my clothes?" But His disciples said to Him, "You see the multitude thronging you and you say, 'Who touched me?'" And He looked around to see her who had done this thing. But the woman fearing and trembling, knowing what had happened to her, came and fell down before Him and told Him the whole truth. And He said to her, "Daughter, your faith has made you well. Go in peace and be healed of your affliction"* (Mark 5:27-34).

This woman's remarkable and profound account showed her to be bound by the "spirit of reduction." Her very life essence had been flowing out for 12 years and nothing was pouring back into her: no joy, no friends, no money, no encouragement, absolutely nothing. She spent everything she had in search of an answer to the issue-of-blood that bound her for 12 long years. Nothing worked and no one could seem to help her. She had spent all her money on the physicians who could not produce any positive results. She became an outcast, simply because she no longer "fit in." Back in the Old Testament days, God's word proclaimed the following:

> *...any menstrual flow that continues for many days beyond the normal period or any blood discharges related to a woman's menstruation makes this woman ceremonially unclean for as long as the discharge continues. The things she sits on, lies upon during that time will be defiled. Any one who touches her bedding too will be defiled.*[2]

Taking this law into consideration, can you comprehend the downward path of this woman's predicament? Being ceremonially unclean, she went through pains of rejection and isolation. No one wanted to have anything to do with her. So, for the most part, her life was one of isolation and she had become a terribly lonely woman. She had no one with whom to share her life: no playmates, no talking pals, and, ultimately, no one to fellowship with. As far as people around her were concerned, she was too needy. Plus, they could not help her because people are weary of those constantly with a need, and who are never truly able to help themselves. Everyone left the woman to her woes. She couldn't touch anything because the law deemed her to be a filthy, social misfit. Her core essence of life was wasting away daily.

With each passing day, she was gradually disintegrating and became more incapacitated, broken, spent, and tired of trying to get an answer. But in all that she was going through, her spirit remained alive and strong and she did not give up in her inner man. She became desperate for a permanent solution to the obviously degenerating offer life had bound her with. She did not plan to spend life that way but it happened nonetheless. She did not negotiate for that portion in life's equation, but it remained something she had to deal with. What did she have left to do? Obviously, she had spent all her time, energy and resources going to the wrong places for answers to her questions. Like this woman, when you come to a grand halt from a deep search for answers to life's threatening questions, what do you do? One thing remains certain, just as she could not find answers from all the places she visited, you cannot find answers for your aching soul outside of God's anointing and presence. You will waste your time, energy, resources, and emotions to look for fulfillment in all the wrong places; when you need definitions for life's situations, the arm of flesh is far too limited to offer a real definition.

Here was a desperate woman who wanted solutions to issues of her life. She had tried her hand on all sorts of methods, but her condition only grew worse. Do you see yourself at all in this woman? Are you empty and wasting away on all sides? Do not be discouraged: darkness may be all around and you are filled with despair but "hold on." The light will soon shine in that tunnel that has trapped you.

One day, amidst her despair, the woman heard about Jesus Christ, the wonderful waymaker who specializes in giving meaning to life when all hope has been lost. He is the One who shows up just before you give up. I am talking about Jesus, the open door: He is the way out of pain and into gain. It is so amazing how you get to hear about Him in the right place and at the right time.

Once this woman heard about Him, her life was never to be the same. Before she came in contact with Jesus, she was at the end of life itself, broken on all sides. Relationally, she stood alone with rejection and her pains are only best imagined. She was financially spent and emotionally distraught. In looking at this woman, I am amazed at her level of spiritual involvement with the Lord Jesus Christ. The crisis went beyond her: she was losing blood daily for 12 years. According to the Law, life is in the blood, so she was dying slowly, losing life from her spirit, soul and body until she met the Man who traded her "life in the blood" with His "life in the anointing."

I am sure she had no beauty to behold at the time. She was not a force to be reckoned with. But one day, she came to herself and realized that there had to be a way out. This is life's punch-line: when life hands you "not enough" and you come to yourself, there is no mountain you can't climb. Suddenly, you become aware of the fact that the Law has no power over you. The Law cannot define who you are because you are operating in a higher realm. The life-giving Spirit is now at work in your mortal body. Oh! It is so sweet to come to yourself and soar in the anointing of the Holy Ghost.

This woman realized that physicians could not handle her ailment because it had defied medical science. If a cure existed at all, she was sure that they would have found it. The physicians' finite wisdom could not comprehend the depth of this ailment, or the depth of God's infinite wisdom and healing power. Going to her family or friends was also pointless. In any case, they had deserted her, because they tired of her. She did not fit into the system and, for that reason, they could not longer handle her. At that point, she realized that this job was one for the Master of the Universe, the Great I Am. With that realization came her search for "the balm of Gilead." In her Spirit, she made connection with Jesus. She had to know that if Jesus did not heal her, no one ever would. When she encountered His presence, her life was awesomely revolutionized right in the midst of despair and frustrations. She fought her way through pressures to get to Jesus, who is the living Word of God. The moment she touched Him—the Word made flesh—virtue flowed from Him to her and she received healing.

When you study that Scripture, you will realize that she was not "cute" about getting to Him. When everyone had given up on her, she did not give up on herself. She was so desperate for her miracle that she fought her way through a maddening crowd to get it. Desperate people will press through the maddening crowd of life to get to Jesus. When you are desperate for Him, nothing can stop you. How desperate are you to touch Him? She was desperate enough to crawl to Him and touch the hem of His garment: the moment she did, virtue flowed from Him to her. You too can experience change when you touch the Word of God because the word is alive and will quicken all dead areas of your life.

"It" Is Not An Issue God Cannot Handle

Many times when we go through tough times in life, we end up looking for our answers everywhere else but Jesus. When we do that, we do not get real answers because the only lasting solutions are to be found in His presence. You cannot find the answers on your job, in your bank account, in a bigger car, and it is not in the arms of someone else—even a spouse—because relationships do come and go. Whatever answers you need are only to be truly found in the presence of our Lord. Look at this woman's courage: in the midst of a massive mob gathered for Jesus, she saw her one chance for a miracle, and made up her mind to touch Him, regardless of the thronging crowd.

She had suffered for so long that she was not about to let His presence slip by merely because of external pressures. She was desperate to touch her solution, and was not concerned about being dignified. Why should she be? This woman was willing to crawl to her miracle. She had absolutely no reason to impress anyone or strive for a fanfare entrance. She needed Jesus and that was all that mattered. She came to Him just the way she was: broken, losing, abused, empty, and an outcast. Heavy with the weight of her obstacle, the multitude pressing in on her, she watches as her stability is crushed. But did that stop her? No, she had tenacity down in her spirit.

When you go through life's threatening situations, do not give in at any point, but hold on to Jesus no matter how bad the crisis may seem. Do whatever you must do to get to Jesus, because when you touch Him with faith, you will be made whole. This woman knew Jesus had it all. It was not easy for her to get to Him because she was weak and bent over from the weight she was carrying. The pressures from the maddening crowd and the protective disciples were hindrances, but she broke down all those barriers and got to Him anyhow. Refuse to let anything intimidate you. Crawl, if you have to, but get into His presence at all costs and experience wholeness. If you are in dire need for solutions to life's issues, get to Him whichever way you can.

Realize that, in life, there will always be obstacles that you will have to walk over. I say this for the simple reason that those who live righteously will suffer persecutions, but these adversities are a stepping stone to a manifestation of more of His glory. The devil is not going to give up on you without a fight. You have to know that the size of your problem isn't an issue any longer. When you come to knowledge of who you are in Christ—and what He accomplished on the Cross so that you enjoy true freedom—you will know that God is more important any problem. No matter what situations may come your way, what go through can never destroy you because you carry His divine presence within you. You are a victor in this life, and can never be a victim, so rid yourself of that "victim mentality." No matter how degrading or humiliating the issue, you are coming out of it. When you resist the temptation of letting circumstances prevent you from getting into His presence, you will actually experience wholeness as you touch Him with faith. As this woman touched the hem of His garment, her withered body was filled with the resurrection power that made her whole. If you can just make it into His presence, virtue will flow from Him to you, quicken the deadness in your life and make you whole.

Where is Your Confidence?

When you come to God, you must come believing that He is all that his Word says He is, and will be that to you as well. Your faithfulness in doing so will be rewarded. He said to Malachi, *"For I am the Lord, I do not change."*[3] He is constant, and remains the same yesterday, today, and forever. Not one iota of His word will change on you, because He is steadfast in watching over His word to accomplish it in your life.[4] There are no short cuts to coming to Jesus: just believe that He is and He will do exceedingly more than we can imagine.[5] There are no questions about His sovereignty, either, because He is absolutely God all by Himself and there is none like Him. He was God from the beginning and will be God even to the end. Do not try to figure out how life is all going to fall into place for you. All you need to do is to cast your cares upon Him and trust Him with your life.

There is absolutely no way our finite minds can comprehend the supremacy of our infinite God, except that He reveal Himself to us. He will not reveal anything to you, if you are not walking in the light of His word because His secrets are only with those who fear Him. With that in mind, come to God for the simple *raison-d'être* that He is worthy of your trust. The carnal mind does not know spiritual things and because God is a spirit, your worship and reverence of Him must be of spirit and of truth. Are you broken, confused and torn apart? How you come to Him does not matter. But be certain that you cannot have an encounter with His presence and still remain the same. In His presences, you will realize that He has not given you the spirit of fear or bondage but of a tranquil mind. When you come believing, you expose that part of your life for a supernatural touch from on high. The crux of the matter is to know that God will be to you in your situations what you know His nature to be, if you do not waver or turn your gaze from Him.

Who Have You Been Listening To?

I was so empty and looking for love and fulfillment everywhere, but from God. I went from pillar to post in search for peace, but none of these people and things I touched brought me any tranquility. I desperately needed a touch from God and I made up my mind to stay on Him when I found out that He is the Prince of Peace. He alone can give us the peace that will bring fulfillment to our lives. When I found out that He is all that mattered as far as inner peace was concerned, I pursued Him with tenacity and focus. It became clear to me that He was all I needed to get to the next level in my life and every next level after that. Ever since I touched him, I have seen His power operate in my life. Yes, I have faced challenges, but no one said life was going to be smooth sailing. Storms will arise as you walk along, but your boat cannot sink because He rests with you inside the boat.

Persecutions, trials and temptations will come, but He has given us the power and authority over all the works of the enemy. We are seated with Him in the realm of the heavens far above principalities and powers.[6] Until we realize who walk in our position of authority, we will constantly live in defeat. The enemy has his agenda and is not going to stop fighting you just because you have come to God. But realize that the devil is not a problem because he is already a defeated foe. All the darts he throws are powerless. Psalm 23 reveals that his fiery darts are only shadows. Know that there is more to walking with God than just getting saved. Satan's darts cannot come near your dwelling place because the rod-and-staff of God are there to comfort you through the storms of life. The devil has no more power over you than you allow him to have. While you know that he is not about to give up fighting you, whom are you listening to?

When I was not listening to God, my life was an upside-down circus. I found myself doing those very things I said I was not going to do, and in the process grieving the Holy Spirit inside me. You have to be very careful who you allow to talk to you. When people tell you all sorts of things, they sow seeds that will germinate ungodly fruit, if you do not guard your heart. It is important to keep your heart with all diligence, because the issues of life spring from your heart.[7] If your heart is laden with junk that your spirit has also been fed, then you stand in danger of getting disconnected from the source of life, which is the Holy Ghost.

You may sometimes think that you are doing it right, but you have a concealed motive and don't even realize it. Somehow, you have not completely yielded all of yourself to God. You find yourself back at the ungodly starting point and then wonder how you ended up there again. Every minute of your life, you are listening to someone: you are either listening to God, yourself, other people. People allow their lives to be dominated by pornographic magazines, thoughts of failure, the lust of the flesh, the love of money, going up the career ladder at any cost and the list goes on. Eventually, they lose sight of what God is trying to do in their lives.

Some people spend hours on the telephone talking about subjects that do not matter one bit. Life is much more meaningful than that. Have you ever thought that every moment of your life should count towards eternity? Your quality of life really matters to God, which is why you cannot afford to be careless. What you allow into your heart is what will eventually come out. To a large extent, whom you are listening to determines the issues that flow out of your life. What, or whom, you listen most often is what eventually dominates your thoughts.

God has called us to pay attention to His word because that is where life exists. We cannot find life anywhere but the Word of God. When you spend time paying attention to God, you will grow into the fullness of His power and anointing. What matters to Him will begin to matter to you. The living Word in your spirit will begin to produce seeds that yield a spiritual harvest. You will not live an average life because you will walk in His excellence. As you behold Him in the beauty of His holiness, your life will grow from one level of glory to another.

Begin to sow right things into your spirit because what you sow is what you eventually reap. The harvest of seeds sown is always much greater than the actual seeds themselves. Once I realized this point, I found it mattered that I sowed right seeds into my spirit because I desired a Godly harvest. Pastor Creflo Dollar once said, “If you don’t like your harvest, change your seed.” You may not like what is happening to you, but it is not too late to change: you can start all over again. You noticed your pattern of doing things, which produce the same results; now, it is time for a major change to take place in your life. Change begins with a firm, inner resolve to submit to the Holy Ghost’s leading and make everything right. Your ways have not profited much, which is why you need to do it God's way. Change will not come by your might or power, but by the Spirit of the Lord.[8]

Moving Too Fast! It is Time to Slow Down

One day, Frank and I were talking about some issues at home. In-between the conversation, Frank interrupted me several times and I got so upset that I eventually withdrew. For much of the day, I refused to say anything to him, in an attempt to practice a healthy expression of anger. Some attempt that turned out to be when, in the actual sense, all I wanted was to have my own way. I thought to myself, "How could he do this? Is he saying that what I had to say was not important?" (Assumptions and thoughts like these, if not nipped in bud, always have a way of magnifying and blowing issues out of proportion.) Later on in the evening, I decided to tell him exactly how I felt about all the interruptions. He said to me, "Lami, you know, you talk so fast all the time, I can hardly keep up with the pace of your speech. In order to get you to slow down, I interrupted you. Because if we were meant to be having a conversation, then both of us should have been involved in the conversation." Right there was a message for me! All my pent-up rage just went out like a deflated balloon.

Many times, we make it to the presence of God, but guess what happens when we get there! We do all the talking. We want to tell Him how bad our situation is and that it isn't working out the way we planned. Simply put, it is always all about us. We want to get "there" at all costs. To the best of our understanding, there is no stopping us. In the meantime, Abba Father is saying "I wish you will just calm down and let us reason together so that I can handle it from that point of weakness. You have come thus far why not relax and enjoy my presence?" Our emotions are running wild and, in the end, we get frustrated with a life we are unable to fix ourselves.

In the calmness and serenity of our soul is when we hear Him out clearly, as He reaches out to take us by the hand and lead us through the paths of quietness and gentility of spirit. Begin to cultivate the attitude of being still in the presence of God. When your thoughts and imaginations are beginning to run wild, you do have the God-given ability to pull down these imaginations, thoughts and strongholds—the ones that have exalted themselves above the knowledge of God—and bring them captive to His obedience.[9] Only once that is done, then you can focus clearly on Him.

Fasten Your Gaze on Him

Lots of obstacles will attempt to stop you from listening to and walking with God. When I talk about listening to God, I mean that your focus is completely on Him, and all distractions are out of the way. You are consistent with the Word, and do not waver even in the presence of contrary evidence. No matter what storms or pressures rise up, you are still found standing on that solid foundation because you know the One called you is able to keep you from falling. When you face a trying time, life will hand you enough reasons to turn elsewhere for succor. But in this walk with Him, you must get to the point of being persuaded that God is able to keep you, even if all around you is falling apart. When you are fully persuaded that He will not allow your foot to be moved, then the anointing can do things which you could not do.

Let Us Walk on Water

When your eyes are fixed on the Lord, even in the presence of contrary evidence, soon enough the supernatural will take over the natural in your life. You will walk on those waters of life—whatever these waters may represent to you—and God will not allow you to sink. You will walk amongst traps set for you by the enemy, but will come out victorious. You will walk over trying situations, but will suffer no harm. God will reveal to you Kingdom principles for gaining mastery over pressures and distractions.

When Jesus beckoned Peter to come to Him while walking on the water, Peter started off with focus. For as long as Peter kept his eyes on the Lord Jesus Christ, he walked on the water. Before long, he became intimidated and overwhelmed—right in the middle of his blessings—and his eyes went off the very core of his stability.[10] "How come Peter missed it"? Ask yourself that question. When God hands you a gift and you focus on the gift more than on Him, you will miss it. Yes, God's blessings are an irrevocable trust, but you will find yourself in a holding mode if you keep your eyes on the gift and not the Giver. Because you took a detour to your destination, you will remain stagnant instead of moving up in your walk with Him. God is constant: we are the ones who change on Him, but He wants us to remain focused and grow into all things that pertain to life and Godliness.

When Jesus asked Peter to come, the disciple stretched out his heart in faith and went along with the Master's command. The moment Peter took his eyes off Jesus, he started to sink. When you lose focus on the Lord, you will sink into the very thing that once had power over you. All He has asked you to do is come, but you must stay focused on Him. When distractions come, don't take your eyes off Him, but just keep walking on water. He is the only One who can keep you from sinking when life's storms come your way. Believe me! The devil will present wonderful opportunities for you to lose focus on God, but you must look forward and keep your eyes on Him. You will have to get to that point where you know that God is in control of everything that concerns you. Be convinced that He is going to use the same issues that threaten your stability to bring you into an intimate relationship with Him. He will keep you for as long as you need to be kept, for He has said, *"When you pass through the waters, I will be with you; And through the rivers, they shall not overflow you. When you walk through the fire, you shall not be burned, nor shall the flames scorch you."* [11]

No one ever said that life was going to be a hassle-free journey. The righteous will suffer persecutions. You will be confronted with trying times. Overwhelming situations will come against you. Many circumstances will show up to distract your attention from Him. But what will determine how well you stand in the face of adversity is the knowledge of His word and how well you are able to apply it. Many times, we are defeated by tragedies because we do not know what the Word of God says concerning those issues of our life.[12] Have you developed your relationship with the Almighty God by the enabling of the Holy Spirit to a level where you are completely sold-out to His word? Because of the living power in His word, your inner convictions will be healthy enough to stay above distractions, pressures and challenges.

As you prosper supernaturally in your spirit, every other area of your life will be linked up in your walk and work with God. *"Dear friend, I am praying that all is well with you and that your body is as healthy as l knows your soul is."*[13] As you daily behold Jesus Christ in the Word of God, you will prosper inside out. Only that knowledge can guarantee how firm you will stand amidst trials and tribulations. This awareness should strengthen you and give you the confidence that even when passing through all these tests, trials and temptations, you will not be overwhelmed or left alone: God has placed you in the seat of authority with power and dominion over all the works of the enemy.

It is absolutely necessary to stay focused because a double-minded man cannot receive anything from the Lord. You need to receive from God: He alone has the answer to what you need on this side of Heaven. Double-mindedness is unbelief and unbelief is pride. Are you shocked at that statement? When you walk in unbelief, you are saying God is incapable of handling your issues, and that you can take care of these issues in your own way, but, in essence, you can't. God alone has answers to questions and gives solutions that no man has ever been able to give you. If you look to Him for help, you will be established. You will not fall because *"those who look to Him for help will be radiant with Joy; no shadow of shame will darken their faces."*[14] Notice it says, those who look to Him: if you are not looking to Him for help, don't expect help to come from Him. Looking to Him means that you turn the eyes of your spirit to His direction in order to see His salvation, concerning issues of your life.

ENDNOTES

1. Mark 5:25-34
2. Leviticus 15:25-27 NLT
3. Malachi 3:6
4. Jeremiah 1:12
5. 1 Corinthians 8:9
6. Ephesians 1:21
7. Proverbs 4:23
8. Zechariah 4:6
9. 2 Corinthians 10:5
10. Matthew 14: 27-31
11. Isaiah 43:2
12. Hosea 4:6
13. 3 John 2 NLT
14. Psalm 34:5 NLT

Soul Search

1. What problems have engulfed you so deeply that you do not believe that there is a way out?

2. Where, what and whom do you resort to for solutions when you are overwhelmed with life's challenges?

3. How confident have you been in God lately?

4. Whom and what do you spend your time listening to?

5. What do you think is responsible for the dissatisfaction in your life lately?

6. What measures will you take to build your confidence in the Lord?

CHAPTER 5

Watch Out For Distractions

In the last chapter, we saw that as long as Peter kept his eyes on Jesus, he walked on water. But Peter started to sink as soon he got distracted and took his eyes off Jesus. He allowed his situation to overwhelm him to the point where he could not see Jesus magnified above the storms. The moment you look away from Jesus and onto the issues confronting you, the whole purpose of your standing on Jesus Christ, who is your firm foundation, will be shaken. At almost every point of your life, you will be confronted with two options: pleasant and unpleasant situations are wrapped up in the cases awaiting you. Which would you rather have? I will give you a sneak preview: good things are supposed to happen to us. Sometimes all may not be okay with your outer world, but what are you going to do with what you are limited to change? The choice is all yours to make. Look at this profound truth in the Word of God:

Today I have given you the choice between life and death, between blessings and causes. I call on heaven and earth to witness the choice you make. Oh, that you would choose life, that you and your descendants might live! Behold I set before you life and death blessing and curses, choose life that you may live.[1]

It is good to know that the decision to choose life is yours to make. When you have x-rayed your life and seen how far you have come, only you can tell yourself the truth. You must be honest with yourself about the choices you have been making and what needs to be done from that point onwards. I know that God is good, because not only did He lay before us life's choices, He went ahead to tell us which to choose. Life may not always present itself the way we planned, therefore comes the need to choose. He has done all He can ever do for us. From now on, the choice is entirely up to us. Look at this amazing Scripture and see the heartbeat of God towards you. The psalmist understood the love of God, both in and out of season, which is why he could say: *"You prepare a feast for me in the presence of my enemies. You welcome as a guest anointing my head with oil. My cup overflows with blessings."*[2]

We can liken the feast prepared by God on His banquet table to life, and the enemies are to be likened to death. Concurrently, with the feast-of-life is going on, you may have hard-core issues to deal with. What do you do then? Which will you chose to focus on? Choose life that you may live. I wish someone could make the choice for you, but that is not possible. At some point, you must make choices of life for yourself. I had constant distractions in my life, but when the Holy Ghost started to expose those areas to me, all I wanted was positive change in the right direction. It became clear that as long as I make the right choices, I could have the best life had to offer amidst all its chaos.

Why settle for average when you can have the best in life? Our challenges may vary, but God's concepts and principles remain the same. When we concentrate on what does not add up to eternal life, we cannot feast on His banqueting table. It is very possible to still be at the top when life's adversities roll in because we are more than a conqueror in all things.[3] If you are sensitive enough to the Holy Spirit's leadings, you can smell the dead rat from a distance. All of it is a trap to keep you from enjoying God's best for you. As we expose these distractions, may there be a shift in your Spirit from dead choices to life-giving choices.

Unbelief!

In life, you can only look to someone you believe in. You may not necessarily see where he is going, but deep down you are convinced that he knows his destination. That conviction about the path he leads enables you to stay with him. That is so true for the God we serve.

> *So you see, it is impossible to please God without faith. Anyone who wants to come to Him must believe that there is a God and that he rewards those who sincerely seek Him.* [4]

Unbelief destroys trust and right relationships. When you have no confidence in the saving power of the Lord, your relationship with Him is not built on trust. Unbelief will cause you to look away from Him and look under the banqueting table for answers; when instead you could sit at the King's table to be served with life's delicacies.

Faith is the prerequisite to believing in Him. Scriptures never give an explanation as to how, or why, we must believe in Him: it simply says, "Believe." You will have to take the step of faith in obedience and believe that He is able to save you, heal you and provide for you. When you take the step of faith, you will see God rise up on your behalf. He will get into the boat with you and you will not sink; for you to sink means that He has to sink. But glory be to God who gives us the victory all the time: He can never sink. If you want to see the promises of God birthed in your life, just trust in Him and keep holding on even when it doesn't seem like the right thing to do. Hold on even if daring pressures are almost choking the joy out of your life. One day you will realize that you got to the finish mark without a scratch, but with a firm resolve to go onto another life's journey with Him. You will be confident that the God, who did it yesterday, is the same God for the journeys of today and tomorrow.

Impatience

The problem with us Christians is that we want everything to happen when and how we want them to. We never stop to find out God's own plans concerning those issues. Do these issues fall within His perfect will for our lives? When we are sensitive to the Holy Spirit, we will learn to let Him lead us through righteous paths. When you are impatient, you really cannot receive from God because you go ahead of Him to fix things for yourself. Do you wonder why you keep failing in life? In his book, *The Leadership Secrets of Jesus*, Dr. Mike Murdock says, "Your greatest mistake will happen because of impatience."[5] While waiting on the Lord, you need time to grow in Him so that you may be strengthened, established and settled.[6] You will learn to be all that God has called you to be. Most importantly, you will know God the way He ought to be known.

Depending on your own understanding will leave you miserable and frustrated because that understanding is limited. The Almighty God's understanding is limitless, which is why you need to hook up with Him as a source. Once you key into Him, His ways will not be past finding out. He knows the end from the beginning; He is able to bring all that concerns you to an expected end. In all you do, trust God, acknowledge Him and let Him have free course in your life. When you do so, He will direct your path. He is eternity itself, therefore, we must get into His time mode and quit trying to accomplish things our way. As you wait quietly and patiently before God, an overwhelming peace will come over you, and your pathway will be directed towards gratifying success. The peace of God that passes all human reasoning and understanding will be your guide. Wait expectantly for Him because He does show Himself strong on the behalf of those whose hearts are perfect towards Him.

What's important to note about turning your impatience to Him is that you will learn endurance and maturity through waiting. An expectant mother does not conceive and give birth to her baby all in the same day. During the nine month waiting period, the baby develops from one stage to another until it gets to full maturity in the mother's womb. When the baby is ready to come out, nothing can stop the baby from coming out at the set time. Why is that? Because the baby must cannot stay in the womb longer than its appointed time. When the due date of my daughter Serita arrived, I knew, without a doubt, that any moment from then, she would be ushered into the world. The very moment the contractions started, I knew nothing was going to keep her in my womb any longer.

The same birth process is true with some of God's promises for your life. Some take a whole while longer to mature before you can birth them. You will carry that promise within you, nurture it, watch it grow and at the right time, which is your season,[7] you will bear your fruits. Once your time has come, you will bring forth that promise in righteousness. At that time, you will know indeed that God's blessings only make rich and add no sorrows. Nothing can stop your moment from breaking forth. But if you go ahead of Him out of impatience, and do things your own way, you will add lots of sorrows to your life. When this happens, you maybe forced to compromise in certain areas of your life. Will you—for the pleasure of a moment—impatiently give in to the pressures of life?

Pain

One of the greatest distractions in the people's lives is pain. In fact, many people are addicted to pain. We live in a world full of pressures and we should be able, with the Holy Spirit's help, to identify what keeps us under. Because they could not medicate their pain with the Word of God, people often engage in acts that they would not have done under "normal" circumstances. If they knew better, they would do better. I have come to understand pain as torments that result from betrayals by loved ones or individuals one had once trusted. Pain can arise from broken relationships, losses and lack, distress, sicknesses, internal and external pressures, physical, mental and emotional abuse. All these can cause distractions, as it is often easy to fix our attention on those painful experiences of past and present.

It is important to treat our pain with the Word of God, otherwise the pain will become an unbreakable barrier, if we hang on to it for too long. This impenetrable barrier will stop the flow of God's word into our hearts. When we look at the hurt and not the Healer, our whole life perspective will be distorted. We become overwhelmed with all we are going through and, before we realize it, we are far gone from our hope of glory. Jesus said, *"Come to me all you who labor and are heavy laden, and I will give you rest."*[8] There is rest in the Lord for all who are burdened. But you can only ever find rest for your aching soul, and the grace to see you through life's ache and pain, by waiting in His presence. Sometimes, the circumstance of your pain is such that you may have to bear it a little longer than you prefer. But what is most important is that, at the end of it all, you will come out a stronger person. I do not promise that all your pains will go away within the twinkle-of-an-eye, but there will be grace available for you to go through it and, at the end, receive rest for your soul.

If your pain is physical or bodily in nature, I want to announce that the Healer, the balm of Gilead, is on His way to your spirit, soul and body. You no longer have to be sick. He took all our infirmities upon Himself so that we can walk in divine health.[9] No matter what ailment you are

presupposition concerning God's plans and purpose. Presuppositions kill dreams and visions, so you need to specifically identify what God desires for you to accomplish here on earth: that way, you can stop making wrong assumptions and taking wrong turns in life.

God knows what our tomorrow holds, which is why we must run the race-of-life with eternity as its focal point. We need to get out of our mind and into the mind of Christ, so we can understand the vision of eternity. We need insight into God's purpose for our lives so we can run the race of life, which God has called us to run. We do not need any human opinion concerning God's call on our lives. We need the Word of God, because the Word is the illuminating source of this life's journey. In this life, you need Christ and His resurrection power to keep on a straight path and avoid distractions. Paul's vision enabled him to remain focused: he did this by devoting his life to knowing Christ. That revelation became the dominant factor of what he did and how he lived. He had quiet a list of achievements and accomplished much in his lifetime. But he came to a point of knowing that none of those accomplishments had given him any real fulfillment and, if he stayed on them, they would still not bring him any peace. Looking at all he accomplished, Paul counted them dung for the excellency of Christ. Like a runner set for a race, Paul kept his gaze on the finish line; he was able to attain his goal because he refused to be distracted. He saw what was ahead of him and refused to give up his crown of glory for momentary pleasures.

Paul refused to put his confidence in the flesh, and he determined to always rejoice—regardless of the circumstances—because he knew that his peace lay in Christ's resurrection power. He certainly had pressures from the external world, but, on the inside, Paul knew himself to be more than a conqueror because the Spirit of excellence and tenacity were found to be fashioned in his character. The apostle had gotten to a place in his walk with God of daily crucifying his flesh for a weightier, greater glory. Secure in the knowledge that he served a God able to exceed his wildest imagination, He did not allow himself to be overwhelmed by any situation. Realizing that true joy comes only from the Lord and not material acquisition or personal accomplishment, he stayed fixed on his goal of knowing Christ.

You need the vision of eternity to be an influencing factor for all you do. Everything on your external world may be falling apart, but you know what lies ahead of this goal, so refuse to get distracted. You must be determined not to allow external pressures to keep you from getting to the finish line. You must refuse the temptation to allow the cares of this world to overwhelm you to the point of losing sight in what you dearly believe in. At the end of life itself, a crown of glory awaits those who get to the finish line. On this side of heaven, your life can only get better because the pathway of the uncompromisingly righteous only shines brighter and brighter unto a perfect day.[12] Keeping your gaze on Him should be your ultimate pursuit in life. Everything else will fade into obscurity and, believe me, nothing will ever give you any meaningful satisfaction. Only your moments with Him will bring you true happiness and contentment. There is absolutely nothing wrong with accomplishment and material acquisition, but setting them as a life's goal is the pathway to un-fulfillment and pain. To put your confidence in the flesh and trust in achievements and accomplishments is to set yourself up for failure in the things of the Kingdom.

Align Your Priorities with the Word of God

Due to his track record and the heights he attained, apostle Paul had every reason to put his confidence in the flesh, but he did not. The list of his accomplishments is an incredible, mind-blowing series of achievements. But he came to a point of realizing how weightless his achievements were in comparison to God's glory set before him. At that point, Paul considered all he had acquired to be mere filth.

> *He was circumcised on the eight day of the stock of Israel, of the tribe of Benjamin, a Hebrew of Hebrews, concerning the law, a Pharisee, concerning zeal, persecuting the church, concerning the righteousness which was of the law, he was blameless.*[13]

Paul knew that to fulfill his calling, his flesh had to lay aside all his had accomplishment, or else they would become a distraction from his destination. (If you understand spiritual matters, you know that no flesh shall ever glory in His presence.)

So Paul aligned his priorities with what God had called him to do. He refused to allow anything he did to be compared with the worth of knowing Christ. The focal point in his spirit was the Lord Jesus Christ. Paul's solid example will make life worth living, if we define what is of "importance." Nearly everything we are chasing after with such tenacity is not as important as we have magnified them to be. Why? For the simple reason, that they do not define our purpose for life. Many Christians go through life without a purpose, which is why they are so miserable and keep going around in circles. Apostle Paul knew his calling and stayed within that jurisdiction. He was not tossed to and fro with the pressures of life, which is why he could boldly say *"... But one thing I do, forgetting those things which are behind and reaching forward to those things which are ahead, I press toward the goal for the prize of the upward call of God in Christ Jesus."*[14]

Apostle Paul was not a jack of all trades, and neither should you be. Stay focused on what the Lord has called you to. You get tossed up and down because you do not realize the need and benefit of holding onto His vision and running with it. You are not fulfilled in life, because you go wherever the tide of life takes you. You deserve much better than allowing life to dictate terms to you. You can have a passion for the Lord and the power of His resurrection. You can wait on the Lord and truly enjoy the benefits of doing so. When you lack vision and purpose in life, you will run to anything in search of fulfillment. But the truth is that you will come out worse off than before.

Only the Lord Jesus Christ can give you true happiness and satisfaction. You cannot find the answer in drugs, money, alcohol and sex or any other vice. After considering all his achievements, apostle Paul concluded that value and satisfaction in his life could only come from being wrapped in Christ and the work He wrought at Calvary. In bringing his vision to fruition, Paul knew that the past had to be let go of. Holding on to your past will be a hindrance for your future. Successes and failures, heights and depths, gain and pain had all been crossed out of his life. Paul started all over again with only one matter grafted on his mind: knowing Jesus and the power of His resurrection. Everything you hold onto has got to go in order to walk in the greatness of Christ for your life. You are going to have to live a life of pressing, pushing and chasing tenaciously after Him. You will have to let go of everything that has kept you distracted so that you can fully understand and walk constantly with God's touch as you continually wait on Him.

ENDNOTES

1. Deuteronomy 30:19 NLT
2. Psalm 23:5 NLT
3. Romans 8:37
4. Hebrew 11:6 NLT
5. *Leadership Secrets of Jesus* by Dr. Mike Murdock: [Pg 162, Copyright 1996, Published by Honor Books, P.O. Box, 55388 Tulsa, Oklahoma 74155].
6. 1 Peter 5:10

7. Psalm 1:3
8. Matthew 11:28 NLT
9. Isaiah 53:3-5
10. Psalm 34:19 NLT
11. Philippians 3:1-14
12. Proverbs 4:18
13. Philippians 3:3-5 NLT
14. Philippians 4:13

Soul Search

1. What issues have you been dealing with that you now know are distractions?

2. What do you intend to do about these distractions?

3. What has caused you great pains and served as source of unforgiveness in your life?

4. Do you have a vision for eternity or do you merely going with the tide of life?

5. Make a list of your priorities. Where does knowing Christ and the power of His resurrection fit into your list?

6. Should you reorder your list of priorities?

7. What commitments will you make to ensure that you adhere to an eternity focused list of priorities?

CHAPTER 6

Desires Engulfed in the Word

Then Jesus was led out into the wilderness by the Holy Spirit to be tempted there by the Devil. For forty days and forty nights he ate nothing and became very hungry. Then the devil came and said to him "If you are the Son of God, change these stones into loaves of bread." But Jesus told him, "No! The scriptures say, "People need more than bread for their life; they must feed on every word of God." Then the Devil took him to Jerusalem, to the highest point of the Temple, and said, "If you are the Son of God, jump off! For the scriptures say, "He orders his angels to protect you. And they will hold you with their hands to keep you from striking your foot on a stone." Jesus responded, "The scriptures also say, "Do not test the Lord your God." Next the devil took him to the peak of a very high mountain and showed him the nations of the world and all their glory. "I will give it all to you." He said, "If you will only kneel down and worship me." "Get out of here, Satan," Jesus told him.

"For the scriptures say, "You must worship the Lord your God; serve only him." Then the Devil went away, and angels came and cared for Jesus[1].

This passage assures me that no matter what I go through in life, there is a way out as long as my desires are engulfed in the Word. I am destined to be above and not beneath, only because I have victory in my spirit. You see, Jesus was tempted in all ways, but He did not fall into temptation. Temptation could come to anyone who is in Christ Jesus, but with every temptation comes an available way of escape. No matter what we do, the intents of our hearts must be wrapped in Him. Temptations come to distract us from our course, but we have the choice to remain focused. The devil tempted Jesus three times and Jesus had an answer ready for him every time. The fact that temptations come to distract you does not make you any less a child of God. The Word of God within your spirit will rise up in that hour of temptation. If nothing is within your spirit, you may not make it through that snare. My heart's desire is that you will store up the Word of God in your heart, so that you are not found wanting when evil days come. The Father's heart desire is for you to rise above the pressures of life.

We have a perfect example in Christ Jesus. He was tempted in every way,[2] but did not give in because He knew the end from the beginning. He didn't need to bow or perform miracles to prove His sovereign identity. He knew exactly who He was and what He was up against. When the tempter came, His spirit was already filled with the Word of God. He did wait until the point of temptation to look for Scripture that would back off the devil. When the storm came, He was already prepared and that was why He did not cave in to pressure. A good soldier always prepares for battles and, therefore, is not taken unawares. If your inner man does not give up, you will definitely win the outer battles. We have been admonished to take up the sword of the Spirit, which is the Word of God.

Swords are meant for battle. When the enemy comes charging, you must have what it takes to arm yourself against his fiery darts. Jesus guarded His heart with the Word because the issues of life are what flow from our hearts. If nothing is inside, then you will have nothing to use as defense when the enemy strikes.

Keeping the Word of God within you is going to take discipline and determination. I remember times when I sat to study the Word of God that, initially, I did not get delight out of, because I saw it as a necessary duty to fulfill all righteousness. Can I be real with you? For any child of God to have such an opinion is laziness to the highest degree. The moment I lined up my heart with His word and the teachings of my wonderful counselor, the Holy Ghost, it became a delight just to get the Word down in my spirit. The *rhema* Word flowed continuously into my heart.

When Frank and I first got married, I had to move from Abuja to our new home in Lagos. I did not get a job within the time frame that I speculated. When I eventually found work, I realized within a matter of weeks that I didn't need all the job-related stress. But I could have avoided that situation had I heeded prophecy from God. Two months before our wedding. I had been discussing with a lady the fact that, after the wedding, I would have to leave Abuja to join Frank in Lagos. At that time, getting a job in Lagos was an issue of great concern. The place where I worked in Abuja did not have a branch in Lagos, so I couldn't get a transfer. A couple of weeks later at church—at the discipleship training school where I served as an assistant—a woman walked up to me and said, " Lami, let me have your notebook. I have a message I want to scribble down for you. Her message informed me that I would be without a job for a while so that I could give my days over to the singular purpose of spending time in prayer and in the Word. When I read it, I said in my mind, "Girl! You must be kidding. What will life be like without a job?"

I had always worked, therefore, I couldn't relate to what she wrote. As a matter of fact, I closed the page of my notebook and pretended that this little discussion never took place. In my mind, I thought, "I can work and still spend time in prayer and the word." After the wedding, I moved to Lagos. Month after month I went out in search of a job, but employment was just not forthcoming. I had so much free time that I did not know what to do with myself. Initially, I felt as if my life was wasting away, and I hated the idea of being at home without much to do. One day, the Holy Spirit ministered to my heart and said, "This is the time to really get rooted some more in the Word. You have no distractions: you should spend quality time in the Word and in prayer daily before your husband gets back home from work." (Don't misunderstand me. I am not saying that your life stops moving when you get married or that God takes away your job. I was simply on an assignment with Him and such a disposition was needful at the time.) Suddenly, I remembered what the lady had written in my book. I felt goosebumps all over me. I thought, "Time in the Word, of course!"

I had been shown a glimpse of what I was supposed to do for a period in time, but I had ignored it. I was literally frustrated for many months because I insisted I had to have a regular job. Somewhere in my mind, I must have equated the regular job with "being somebody." That mindset had to broken. Regular job or none at all, I had to know that I am precious in the Father's eyes. I had to know that the Word of God defines me, and not gainful employment. I had to know that I am accepted by the Beloved. I quickly repented for not delighting in the time made available so that I could give myself over to studying the Word and being in prayer. At times, I had difficulties sitting for hours at a stretch in study because all sorts of distractions weighed around me.

But as I continued to press forward, my study life graduated from being a duty to a delight. At all costs, I made up my mind to submit to

in the Word is unmistakably proved strong when you do not cave in when faced with trying challenges.

Know that the enemy will not give up without a fight. As often as possible, satan will come to distract you. The devil wants you to follow his agenda for your life rather than that of God. For this reason, you should be on the alert at all times and guard your heart diligently before he strikes. Armed with the Word, you will be well able to take him down when he strikes. In Christ Jesus, you have all power and authority to trample over the works of the enemy. Many people lose God's purpose for their lives out of a false belief that life is all about satisfying carnal desires. They are always up in God's face only for what they can get from Him and not for who He is. Jesus hit this point straight home when He said *"it is written, Man shall not live by bread alone, but by every word that proceeds from the mouth of God."*[5] There is more to life than letting our desires run wild. If you have to satisfy every craving thrown at your by the flesh, where and how do you think you will end? The devil knows full well that mankind's desires are insatiable. Bringing all your desires under subjection of the Holy Spirit will give your life much more meaning.

True Satisfaction

True satisfaction in life comes from total commitment to the Creator and not the creation. Commitment does not come overnight, but when you continue working on your relationship with God, and obey Him in all that He has asked you to do. When you purpose in your heart to live a life worthy of His praise, the reverential, worshipful fear of Him will not allow you to pursue your desires. In working out this relationship, you need to be dedicated to His way of doing things. Along with that, you must sacrifice to Him at the altar what you would have otherwise preferred to do. What should matter most is where you are going in this life with God on your side, and what He is going to accomplish through you.

When you commit to a life-pleasing that's to God, you will go through many adverse situations, but God will always be there for you. He will be an ever-present help in trouble and deliver you through it all. Sometimes you hope that God will deliver you from the pressures, but it may not necessarily happen that way. You will see God pulling through the storms, and sometimes He delivers you outright. When temptations, trials and distractions seem so strong that you want to give in, look up to Jesus and strength will flow from Him to you. Remember that the devil only wants to block God's wonderful plans and purposes for your life. He wants to distract you from the glorious end that God has for you. If you do not understand God's purpose for your life, you will live a life of compromise. What you need to do is find out God's purpose for your life and then live it.

His purpose is a high calling. Therefore, you must understand who you are in Christ and what He has called you to do. Live the life he's called you to so that you are not found working with the wrong motives. It is a terrible thing to get to a journey's end only to realize that you haven't even begun. Your failure in destiny will be for the singular reason that you spent an entire lifetime doing the right things at the wrong times and for the wrong reasons. As you spend moments waiting on Him, you will fully understand what it means to consistently lean on the Holy Spirit for every step, and then watch Him take you from glory to glory. You will know what to do because He will order your every step.

Letting your inner desires be for His presence is all a part of waiting on the Lord. As you become enamored with His presence, His glory will rub off on you. Your character and integrity gets built up. Pressures and storms of life will not dismay you. When your soul and inner desire thirst for the living God, then you will be made whole. You may never be able to answer some questions about life, but you will not be afraid to trust Him because your times are in His hand. You may have compelling reasons to be disquieted within, but when you remember that lifting up comes in His presence, you will press on toward the mark for the price set before you.

Doing It Right But Still Hard-Pressed On All Sides

The temptations of Jesus Christ showed Him to be human like you and I are, and that makes it able for Him to identify with our frailties. Why would the Son of God go through all these tests and trials you might ask yourself? Well, these temptations were stepping stones for the glory of God to be revealed through Him. Remember that everything you are going through today is a stepping stone for a higher walk in glory. Realize that after He was tempted of the devil, the angels of God came and ministered to Him. It may look like you are hard-pressed on all sides but hang on: a greater dimension of ministration awaits you right from the throne room of grace. If Jesus Christ faced all He did without giving up, then you can go through life and not give up too. We do not need to be dismayed when we face temptations because the temptation itself is not the sin. Yielding into temptation is the sin. When we choose to yield to temptation, we have automatically chosen to walk in disobedience. God rejects disobedience, which comes with a curse. We are only blessed when we walk in obedience.[6] We have the Holy Spirit of God dwelling inside, so if we allow Him to lead us then we will not gratify our desires. He gives us power to say "Yes" to God and "No" to the devil.

For God made Christ, who never sinned, to be the offering of our sin, so that we could be made all alright with God through Christ.[7]

When we look at what Jesus did on the Cross, we do not need to fear the world's system: even though we are in the world, we are not of this world. We have been given a place of higher authority in Christ. We are seated with Him in heavenly places and that is where we operate. Yes, the work wrought at Calvary has given us right-standing with God. We must be sensitive enough in our hearts to allow the Holy Spirit to lead us into this truth. We have the power to live above standards that the world has placed for humanity. When we remember that Christ became our hope of glory because He was made a sin offering for us, we should put sin where it belongs.

> *Then Jesus was led up by the Spirit into the wilderness to be tempted by the Devil.*[8]

In pondering this Scripture, I wondered, "Why did Jesus have to be lead into the wilderness to be tempted? Temptations did not come to Jesus Christ when He was out with His disciples preaching, teaching and healing people, or when he was feeding 5,000 with two loaves and five fishes, or when he was giving Peter a net-breaking catch of fish, or even when he was out washing His disciples' feet. To sum it up, Jesus was not tempted when all seemed alright in His external world and He was doing His father's business. When all around you seems calm and you are walking in the Holy Ghost's power and anointing, the devil may not show up. But you still have to be very sensitive to his stratagems and, at all times, pray in the Holy Ghost, who happens to be the exact Person who led Jesus into the wilderness.

What are you going to do if you are in wilderness experience allowed by the Holy Ghost? Are you going to sink in despair, or hold steadfast onto the One able to keep you from falling, until you see His salvation? You never have to be afraid because the Holy Ghost is our wonderful counselor. I have learned that the greater the test, the greater the victory, because to whom much is given, much is expected. When you are slain under the anointing, worshiping and praising God, do not expect the adversary to show up. The enemy arrives when you have been pulled aside, and everything has been stripped away, and you are faced with a decision to make. Like Job, you come to your wit's end and you want to throw in the towel and walk out on God: although you have called on Him, the silence is driving you up the wall. You are overwhelmed, tired, lonely, confused and in need of direction. You feel incredibly vulnerable. Now this is not to be condemning you, but if you lack patience and endurance, then the enemy will capitalize on that as well. God has already gone ahead and told you what to do.

We need to be sober, calm and alert because the adversary will not tempt us beyond our physical, emotional and material needs. That is where the lust of the eyes, the lust of the flesh and the pride of life come into play. When you get to the end of your rope, then that is the time to rise up on the inside, because God's strength is made perfect in our weakness. He does not need your strength to pull you out of that hole, but He does need your confidence in Him. If you can wait on Him one more day, one more hour, one more minute, or one more second, I guarantee that the Son of Righteousness will arise with healing in His wings[9] on your behalf.

Determination: The High Road to Living Above The Stratagem of The Enemy

When you are expected to make certain decisions under pressure, you must do so in a circumspect fashion. Be determined by the power of God to not make decisions when in an emotional extreme. As you continue to wait on the Lord, your emotions will be brought under control of the Holy Spirit. He identifies with your struggle, so the Lord can very easily step into your issues. He was tempted in every way but never gave in to the devil's agenda, so that gives Him an inside track on our situations. Redemption for us would have been a forgone issue had Jesus Christ given in to the tempter. Praise be to God who gives us the victory in all things, and Jesus was victorious to the very end. He was so victorious that, "even death could not hold him down."

God has much He wants to accomplish through you, but you must be very careful of what you take into your spirit. The Spirit of Christ Jesus dwells in us, and He has given us victory so we never have to bow to the god of this world. In many ways, the devil sets out to tempt us with what we have taken for granted, along with what we have not completely handed over to the Holy Spirit. Satan will always try to use what you desire most to satisfy your cravings, which is why you have to watch out for your desires. What do you dwell on? What matters most to you? Whom do you spend time talking to, listening watching and reading? If your desires are not aligned with the Word of God, the old serpent will get you to do the right things for the wrong reasons.

God put desires in us and it is perfectly normal to have them. But hear this, the psalmist instructs us to delight ourselves in the Lord. If you are not delighting yourself in the Lord, you will have reason to delight in other things. One of the promises in the Word is that *"a broken and a contrite heart—these, the Lord will not despise."*[10] Do not try to manipulate God with your desires. If your desires are acting up, then access the presence of God to walk in purity of heart. He will create a clean heart and renew the right spirit within you. It is a terrible to come before God with selfish motives because they are a set up for failure. This is where determination to stay above the enemy's wiles comes in. When your desires are properly aligned with the Word of God, the devil can try you, but he won't succeed because the greater One lives within you.

Your need to spend quality time in God's presence should remain consistent, because life will always present attractive, persuasive reasons as to why you should try something else for fulfillment. At times, life presents uncertain choices that may seem to be a better option, even when you already know the right thing to do. Praying always and staying in the Word of God will help you realize God's standard for living. Only when you understand the Lord's counsel will recognize foul stratagems from the enemy's camp. I will reiterate the fact that you cannot do without the Word of God in your life. When moments of pain, distraction, lack, decision-making, and need come upon you, the Word of God stored within your heart—along with wisdom to apply it—will rise up from within.

Remember the tale when Daniel[11] purposed in his heart not to eat the foods set before him by King Nebuchadnezzar. He had no trouble standing firm on his decision because his mind was already made up. He did not wait to get before the king before making a decision. Do like Daniel did, and do not wait for storms to come before you have chosen what to do. Get the Word of God into your heart so you what He is saying when storms come. As Jesus overcame, so you too can overcome, because we look up to our High Priest, the Apostle of faith and the Author of truth. Whatever the circumstance might be—a wilderness experience or a temptation straight from the enemy's camp—you have what it takes to overcome and get into the Promised Land. The answer to everything comes by waiting in His presence.

CAN I COMPREHEND HIS SILENCE?

Apostle Paul prayed concerning the thorn in his flesh (in 2 Corinthians 12). He wanted the thorn out of his life so bad that he pleaded three times for God to remove it. At some point, He must have thought that God did not hear Him. Some answers from God come at the "snap" of fingers, but others do not. No matter how early or late your answers show up, God heard the moment you lifted that issue up before Him in prayer. You must have that much confidence in your prayer life.

And this is the confidence (the assurance, the privilege of boldness) which we have in Him: [we are sure] that if we ask anything (make any request according to His will, in agreement with His own plan), He listens to and hears us. And if (since) we [positively] know that He listens to us in whatever we ask, we also know [with settled and absolute knowledge] that we [granted us as our present possessions] the requests made of Him.

The thorn in your flesh may be bothering you, and be such a hindrance that you cannot do what you love to do in life. You are desperate for an answer, but the shocking revelation you get is more of His silence as you continue praying. While you were yet praying, He heard you. His silence is a process for the manifestation of the great glory to be revealed through you. You must have the conviction within your spirit that He heard your prayer, even if you do not see an immediate response. Yes, it may look as if the situation has not changed since you started knocking on Heaven's doors. But remember that when all is quiet from above, God is working out a far exceeding weight of glory for you. There were times when I prayed for certain things to happen, but the results did not come when I wanted them to. I stayed up late hours into the night seeking His face for immediate answers, but did not receive any. However, I prayed knowing that because He has loved me with an everlasting love, He will not suffer my foot to be moved. When I approached His presence with this confidence, it was only a matter of time before He showed up strong on my behalf.

There was a reason why the thorn was not removed from our dear apostle Paul immediately after he prayed: it was not that God was not aware that the thorn existed. He knew all about it and He heard all of apostle Paul's prayers. Perhaps, God would have taken it away, but he chose to leave it there for a reason. The "thorn" must have been for apostle Paul's good that He left it there to pummel him. Approach God with the confidence that as you wait on Him, everything is going to be all right. Be confident that no matter how long it takes, your answers will show up in His presence. Every valley in your life will be filled, all the crooked places will be made straight and every mountain will be brought low.

You must develop confidence in Him, and not lose focus in His supreme ability over your limitations. The prophet Habakkuk experienced some hard times, but he did not change on God. Even though it seemed like God was far-fetched, he built his confidence in the Lord to a point where he could boldly say, *"Though the fig tree may not blossom yet...will I rejoice in Lord."*[12] The world around him was falling apart, and he was going through a rough and difficult time. But he stood on his confidence that no matter what happened, God was faithful to get him through it.

You may not see much happening outside, but the Lord has heard your cries and He will show up in His own special way. All you need to do is to stay focused. Refused to be shaken or bent out of shape because of pressures. If the experience is for a good cause, you will go through it with a lot to learn, but you will not be moved. You have the grace upon your life to walk in His steps and experience victory in the final outcome. There should be within you a knowing about God's faithfulness upon those who wait on Him. You cannot make your relationship with God be casual, but rather be confident that He will give to you your heart's desires. He always faithfully rewards those who diligently wait on Him. You have to wait for Him and know that He will show up at the right time. While you wait, I encourage do not to give up, cave in or quit because His grace is sufficient for you.

His Ability Shows Up When We Are at Zero Level

My grace is sufficient for you and my strength is made perfect in weakness.[13]

Life presents overwhelming complexities and you pray for a way out, but then nothing seems to happen. You ask yourself, "What do I do?" But you pray and ask all you can, but the answers seem far-fetched: all you get is silence. You could almost hear a pin drop in that silence. "Where are you God?" That is your cry of despair. You have pleaded, yelled, cried, prayed, fasted, but still nothing happens. The gnawing silence is tearing your heart apart—you just don't understand it any longer. You are so desperate to hear Him say something. You thought that if you did all He asked, then every line would fall into its perfect place. You have done all you are expected to, but the one thing you wish would happen to remains far away from your reach. Tired of feeling those pains, you wish the temptations wouldn't come your way. All you want is for the hurt to just disappear.

You will do anything to get your situation changed and then, finally, in the quietness of your soul, you hear Him say, "My grace us sufficient!" Now you wonder, "Does God really care? Is He really out there? Does He know what I am going through?" When you are done with all your questions? You still hear Him say, "My grace is sufficient for you." Such an experience offers lessons you are learning that will take you and keep you in the next level of life. You need to have an experience of victory in your walk with the Lord. As you go through life, what is happening to you daily is called "dependability" on God. You get to a point where you trust completely in Him, become steadfast in the ways of the Spirit and rely on Him consistently, whether situations work out the way you want them to or not. The fact that you cannot change anything is indicative of God's supremacy over your natural limitations. He is all encompassing in His ability, which is why you must wait on Him. If you could change the circumstances you were passing through all by yourself, you would have done so by now.

You have to wait and see the salvation of God in your situation. Waiting on the Lord is all about patience, and the ability to go through a hold-up, interruption, aggravation or pressure without complaining and giving up. Looking at Jesus Christ, our example, He endured the shame on the Cross for the glory set before Him. There is need for endurance when you are going through wilderness experiences in life. Such experiences keep you humble, and remind you of the stable need to contact God daily. When you have to go to God all the time, you will be aware of your inability and His ability in you. People have lost patience with God because they want "right now answers" and God is saying, "Wait on me and see my saving power."

A Work Towards Maturity

> *Dear brothers and sisters, whenever trouble comes your way, let it be an opportunity for joy. For when your faith is tested, your endurance has a chance to grow. So let it grow, for when your endurance is fully developed, you will be strong in character and ready for anything.*[14]

God has been so patient with us, but we have often tried to get ahead of Him. We simply need to know that God is working out certain things in us for our good. In those hours when we do not understand his silence, what He is working out in us will come to maturity. We will only get frustrated when we attempt to get ahead of Him. With God, it is one step at a time and that is why the Scripture tell us about *"the path of the just that shines brighter and brighter unto a perfect day"* (Proverbs 4:18). You need patience in your walk with God because He alone knows the road to where you are going. If you go ahead of Him, you will miss your turning points in life. He has told you about the final outcome, but you need to walk with Him in trust, obedience and confidence until you get to that final destination. You need patience with people too. Because you make contact with day-to-day life, people will come in and out of your life for multiple reasons. If you do not learn how to handle your relationships with people, you will drive yourself up the wall.

Some time ago, my sister Kai lived with me, and I had the time of my life with her. I was dogmatic about how I wanted the house kept. If anything was displaced from the position I put it in, Kai was sure to hear about it from me. I would go on and on about how prim-and-proper the house must be. Believe me, it was a frustrating because Kai was not that sort of a person. She would rather relax in the house and not be bothered about "Lami's perfectionist tendencies." It took a long while, but I had to learn to let Kai be her own person. If she wanted the cup to be on the table, then so be it.

Months later, after many ruffles as to what should be kept where, I came to realize that we must make healthy sacrifices in life so as to live in peace. Gradually, it did not matter to me if the cup was on the table or in the cupboard. Through many frustrations, and finally giving up, I learned to be patient with Kai. Not having to follow my self-made, inflexible, regimented house rules made for a lighter burden. I must have driven myself crazy several times before I came to understand that everything, and everyone, in life will not always be the way we want them to be. This is particularly true of the people whom God has put in our lives life for various types of relationships. I also remember other times when I pushed my self over the edge. Whenever I had visitors at home, I just couldn't relax and enjoy their presence. Why? Because I was busy looking over my shoulders or down at my feet to be make sure that no one spilled anything on the carpet. More often than not, the visitors are barely out of the house before I am busy straightening things up. Why should I heap all that pressure on myself?

You must take time to study and understand the people whom you are involved with and why they do the things they do. If you do not get to the point of realizing that people will be inconsistent, you will become schizophrenic in life. You may want people to be what you want them to be, but the truth is that people do change. The only one who will not change on you is God. He told Malachi, *"I am the Lord your God. I do not change."* Do you see why your trust must be in Him alone? He alone is constant. Understand that life's challenges are but a preparatory ground for a higher, deeper walk with the Holy Spirit. When you go through them, you come out a better, more mature person.

Finally, you need to be patient with yourself. As the development of your persona becomes the building block of your existence, you need to watch out for that which constitutes your character formation. Knowing full well that character is the reality of who you are when no one is looking, be sure to remain consistent in your dealings with God and man. At times in life, you may so desperately want to compromise because that seems to be the only way out. But then you will hear Him saying, "My grace is sufficient for you." As you spend a time-of-refreshing in God's presence, He will reveal Himself to you and grant you understanding of His Word. Then as you appropriate that Word in your life, your character will get developed to the point where you will make right choices. I am talking about choices that are decent, upright, honest, sincere and proper, even when no one is observing you.

Father, Let This Cup Pass Over Me

There must have come times in your life when you wanted your "cup" of issues to pass over. You almost wish there were alternative ways of getting to the end of these issues. I have passed through those times when all I wanted to do was walk away from issues. Little did I fully comprehend that the One who holds the world in His mighty hands was watching over me. The desire to leave was so strong, but somewhere in my spirit, I knew that my tenacity in His presence was going to get me to the next level. You have been trying and are tired of doing so; all you want to do is throw in the towel. You have prayed, *"Father let this cup of suffering pass over me."*[15] You may never be able to understand why it seems that He is quiet on you, but it is noteworthy that you have His attention in all that silence.

Keep registered on your mind that even when you face trials, and pass through overflowing waters and scorching fires, God does have you in the palm of His hands. He will not let any evil come near your dwelling place. He is watching over you and glory will flow from Him to you in the midst of a storm. You will never sink in despair, because He will not allow your foot to be moved. The more silence He presents, the more you learn about patience and endurance. The reason God doesn't bring you out of certain circumstances as fast as you want is because He has you in the middle of a class where meaning is being added to life. Bringing you out prematurely will cut the class short before the lesson is finished. When your staying power and resilience are fully matured, you will burst forth from that class like a wellspring of life into everlasting joy. He may not do and say everything you want, but understand that no matter what is going on in your life, you are in a training school with a degree awaiting you when the course ends.

It Is Time to Get the Anointing Out of You

The training school is where the anointing is released from you. The anointing oil is a type of the Holy Spirit: its ingredients are 500 shekels of myrrh, 250 shekels of sweet smelling cinnamon, 500 shekels of cassia and an hin of olive oil.[16] Based on their characteristic features, myrrh, cinnamon, cassia and olive oil represent different stages of our walk with God. Myrrh is a dried gum from the bark of a ragged, low prickly plant that grows in East Africa and Arabia; it is a perfumed gum with bitter taste, which is used as an embalming substance. Myrrh signifies those dry stages of life when you have prayed and nothing seems to be happening. You can almost taste the bitterness of the extended wait. When it looks as if nothing is ever going to happen and there seems to be no way out, you suddenly discover that your best is realized in this "dry stage." In this wilderness experience, all the garlic, leaks, onions and cucumber get taken away and are replaced with trusting God for every provision. At this stage, the Holy Spirit embalms everything not of God from your life. The perfume in myrrh signifies the sweet aroma about you once the flesh has been embalmed. You have come to that point where *"he must increase and you must decrease."*[17] You do not hold strongly onto anything on this side of Heaven because "self" has been embalmed so that Christ may reign supreme in you.

The presence of cinnamon, a highly priced, sweet-scented cane, creates attractiveness in you. Notice that you only need half as much the quantity of myrrh to nullify the bitterness you might have encountered in life. Cinnamon is a reflection of your life's worth and value when all is said and done. I have been through stages in my life where it looked as if there was no hope, but I waited on Him even when bitterness filled my mouth. When situations in my life were going through an embalming process, I waited on Him and then came the anointing.

The Holy Anointing

> *And you shall command the children of Israel that they bring you pure oil of pressed olives for the light to cause the lamp to burn continually.*[18]

You are the light of the world. The anointing upon your life is supposed to make your light shine. You couldn't have gone through the process of mixing the anointing oil's ingredients and not come out pure, ready to shine into His excellence. The truth is that your oil must be pure. If you pour impure oil into the lamp of your life, your light will shine unsteadily. You are the anointing—the oil that causes the lamp to shine—

so how do we get the pure oil out of you? It gets extracted by going through the process of squeezing and mixing the ingredients within different stages of your walk with God. You taste all its stages and do not get overwhelmed because anointing gets released through the process. You passed through the troubled waters, but were not overwhelmed. You went through the fire, but did not even smell like smoke. When the process is over and done with, you are to be put in a holy place. You can no longer be put into any place, go anywhere you like, or keep looking at whatever your eyes want because you are of a holy anointing. In all do you, holiness is a factor because He says *"be holy for I, the Lord your God, am holy."*

Where Are You Right Now?

It may seem that you are at the very bottom of life and all it has to offer, but you will not be there for long. As a child of God, your position in life is "above only and not beneath." You are created to be the head only and not the tail. You have no business being at the bottom, so what are you doing at the bottom? You must come up to where the eagles soar high. When you are up high in the spirit, everything else lies beneath you, including that very pressure which keeps you awake all night long. When you look out from an airplane flying at its top altitude, the scenery beneath you looks ever so small. You see, when you gain an altitude in the Holy Ghost, everything will pale in comparison to your height in Him. Your wife may have walked out and left you wondering what happened to that love once shared. Not long after that, the doctor wrote you off: He gave you a diagnosis of "no cure" and only two months to live. Your bank account reads "zero" and you have no idea where your next meal is coming from. Whatever scary situation may have presented itself to you, our Ever-Present Help in trouble says, "Hang on! Change is on the way." When I come to my wit's end, I walk through the path of His faithfulness and realize that there is nothing concerning my life which He cannot handle. Recount God's faithfulness from time past and see that He can handle your present situation.

Consider the widow of Zerapheth, who needed an infilling from God on her emptiness.[19] If God had not come through, the rest of her tale might have been wiped out of the Book of Chronicles. But the ever-faithful God touched her. When her cruse of oil and bin of flour had almost run out and she had no idea where to get the next supply, He showed up right on time. The God who is more-than-enough gave her an abundance of flour and oil, and that gift completely transformed her life. When Jonah was in the dark pit of the fish's belly, he cried out to the God of the heavens and the earth and He spoke to the fish. The Lord went past the belly of the fish (which was an internal conflict for Jonah) and past the waters (an external conflict) and had the fish spew Jonah out of its mouth.[20] Whatever your conflict is, He can bring you out.

Only remember that *"those who observe lying vanities forsake their own mercy"* (Jonah 2:8). Anything you do outside of faith and trust in God is a "lying vanity." He came through for the Shunammite woman, and raising her son from the dead. [21] When Daniel was thrown into the lion's den, He showed up to shut the mouths of these ravenous jungle beasts.[22] Are you at a point in life where you need the mouths of some lions around you to be shut? Don't observe lying vanities. The God of Daniel is still the same God today. Talk about divine presence and providence: He sent down manna from heaven and fed the Israelites when they were in the wilderness.[23] Talk about bringing life back to a dead, rotten, and stinking situation: He raised Lazarus from the dead after he had been buried in a tomb for four days.[24] Again, He caused Peter to have a net-breaking catch of fish when the disciple had no idea where the next fish would come from.[25] When Paul and Silas were in prison, they prayed for release: then the walls shook and God brought them out.[26]

No matter where you are when God gets ready to bring you out, He will shake the walls that have had you bound. He will break open doors of opportunities for you that no man can shut.

It is not that God doesn't want to give you things; for He created them and they are His to give out. The only problem is that it dishonors His sovereignty whenever we are up in His face asking Him to give us things, instead of asking for Him and the power of His resurrection to be made manifest in our lives. There is so much more to Him than a "give me, give me list." Whatever happened to putting your trust in God? Who ever said that the way up is without hitches? You know that the devil will not give up without a fight, but thanks be to God who gives us the victory through Christ Jesus. How else do you know—in the midst of your crisis—that He is the Alpha and Omega, the beginning and the end of all things that concern your life? How else do you know him as your Ever-Present Help in trouble, the One who releases the anointing out of you in the midst of bitter and troubled waters?

You need to know that He displaces mountains, making streams in the desert and islands on the sea. Whatever the mountain, stream or island represents to you, He will perform a leveling and filling-up of the mountains and streams. He will place you where He designed for you to be. God will give solutions to your predicaments His own way because our own ways cause us to be troubled. We have to lay down our plans at the altar of sacrifice, and burn them up so His glorious plans will descend to us from "our thousand burnt offerings of yielding to His plans." Regardless of where you are coming from or think you are going, it only matters to know that *"all things work together for good to those who trust him."*[27] God's plans for us are the best. We need to align our priorities with His. We need to get the point of telling ourselves that it is a time of giving up all to Him.

GIVING UP TIME

But seek first the kingdom of God and His righteousness, and all these things shall be added unto you.[28]

Your Heavenly Father knows what you have need of, but you won't get far in His presence when you lose you patience and throw an emotional tantrum. When all things come to a screeching halt in your life, you need conviction from within that God knows all about it and that He is doing something on your behalf. At the set time, He will show up. When He does, it will resemble when the Lord brought back the captivity of Zion, and they were like those who had dreamed.[29] The return from captivity was a joyful experience, as He literally turned their lives around: it happened so suddenly that they appeared to be dreaming. When you let go, give up the worry and begin to earnestly seek His face, and not His hand; He will bring you to the point so you know that the hand of the Lord brought you out. As you make the march into your freedom, you will be filled with laughter and sing to the Most High.

At certain times in our lives, situations have happened to cause us to feel as though God has left us alone. But that is an absolute lie: His Word says that, *"He would never leave us nor forsake us"* (Hebrews 13:5). Often times, we get obsessed with what is staring us in the face, and we become ignorant of His providence. We must get to that place of knowing that no matter what the devil dumps on us, God has planned our way-of-escape: we will come out if we put trust in Him. Father God is waiting with outstretched arms to take us to that rock that is higher than we are. All along, you held on to your own ways of doing things and, alas, none of them brought you much gain. Let go, so that God will take preeminence in everything that concerns you. If the One who created you and all creation knows that you have these needs, then isn't it only divine for Him to care for you. He wants you to completely trust in Him and not put confidence in your previous ways of operating.[30] Once you search for His presence, your life will take a different dimension.

In his book *God's Eyeview*, pastor Tommy Tenny says, "When you link magnification of God with proximity or closeness to him, he fills up your whole screen so that all you see is him."[31] The Father already knows you have needs, but He wants you to come seeking *Him* first. When He becomes enthroned in your life, you will know Him as all that really matters. When God gets ready to move you out, He will shake nations on your behalf; He will reach out into where there is lifelessness, and break down walls and barriers just for you. In the face of contrary evidence, you still have to believe Him. Trusting in Him means to give up worrying. You have to decide that nothing on this side of Heaven is worth losing sleep over. God knows it all: He heard your desperate cry and is on His way to your issues. As you give cheerfully to Him,[32] of your heart, time, substance, worship and prayer in the face of pressure, He will *not* abandon you.

ENDNOTES

1. Matthew 4:1-11NLT
2. Hebrew 4:15
3. Joshua 1:8
4. Deuteronomy 8:2-5 NLT
5. Matthew 4:4
6. Deuteronomy 28:2-14
7. 2 Corinthians 5:21 NLT
8. Matthew 4:1
9. Malachi 4:2
10. Psalm 51:17

11. Daniel 1:8
12. Habakkuk 3:17,18
13. 2 Corinthians 12:9
14. James 1:2-4 NLT
15. Matthew 26:39
16. Exodus 30:22-25
17. John 3:30
18. Exodus 27:20
19. 1 King 17:8-16
20. Jonah 2:1-10
21. 2 King 4:8-37
22. Daniel 6:10-23
23. Exodus 16:1-36
24. John 11:38-44
25. Luke 5:1-11
26. Acts 16:24-28
27. Romans 8:28
28. Matthew 6:33
29. Psalm 126:1-6
30. Proverbs 3:5
31. *Gods Eyeview*, (Copyright 2002 by Tommy Tenny, Thomas Nelson Inc., Nashville, Tennessee, p. 138.)
32. 1 Corinthians 8:9

Soul Search

1. How do you stand when temptations, trials, test and pressures come against you?

2. Do you easily sink into pressures with despair? Does the Word of God rise from within when you are pressure points?

3. How do you delight yourself in the Lord?

4. Do you take advantage of His Grace or do you misuse it?

5. What do you have to say about your character development?

6. How do you react when you think that God is silent?

7. What are you doing about "the cup" that looks as if it will not pass over you?

CHAPTER 7

A Personal Knowledge of the One You Are Waiting Upon

Most fundamental to your walk is a personal knowledge of the Lord God. What does He mean to you? What is you relationship with Him like, and are on a one-on-one level? It is an honor to wait on the Lord, but you cannot wait on one whom you have no knowledge of. Scripture asserts the reality of God's supremacy: He is God from the beginning[1] and He reigns throughout eternity. He has chosen to make Himself known to us by revelation in our spirit man. These revelations come to us by faith as we spend time in His presence. The degree to which you spend time with Him is the degree that He will reveal Himself to you. Until you develop a relationship with Him, there are levels and depths you otherwise would not know. He wants you to live in the reality of His persona. When we come before Him, our focus should be to have an intimate relationship with Him. We must yield ourselves completely to Him, and love Him with all we have from the depths of our spirit, soul and body.

He wants us to know Him by His name just as He revealed Himself to Moses.[2] The name of the Lord is an encompassing name that enlightens us about as to His nature, and serves as a total revelation of His character and personality. Having accomplished all he had, apostle Paul said, *"That I may know Him and the power of His resurrection"* (Philippians 3:10). We have to know Him in our lives. He is everything to us: but until we know that fact, we will continually live below His standards set for us in His all-encompassing name. Throughout Scripture, He revealed Himself in so many ways. I have chosen to share a few revelations that show who and what He is. I urge you to dig deeper in Scriptures for a greater revelation of His personality.

He is...

He is Our Shepherd,[3] the one who watches over us in our journey through life. His nature is to guide us through our walk and comfort us when life threatens to be overbearing. He is always there for us, so that we do not sink into despair.[4] He is an ever-present help in times of trouble. He is the only one who will never leave nor forsake us. He is the one who brings peace to our soul when life's storms roll over us.[5] He will always keep us in perfect peace when our mind is stayed on Him. What could be more rewarding than having the God-kind of peace, which surpasses our human reasoning?

He is the Lord who will provide for us.[6] We cannot suffer lack because God is in the business of providing for His children. When the Israelites roamed the wilderness, He provided manna from Heaven, so their candles never dimmed and they never went to bed hungry. Now what about those of us in a covenant relationship with the Lord Jesus Christ? There is absolutely nothing He cannot do. He is the Lord who triumphs, and assures us victory in our life's battles.[7] We have to know that the battle belongs to the Lord's and that there is no need to fight battles for Him.

When pressures of life hit you, keep your eyes on the Lord who has already given you victory. When you fall short of the mark, the Lord is there to sanctify you,[8] although His sanctification is not license for you to keep falling into sin. He forgives your past, present and future sin. Why wait on a list of rules when you can wait on the everlasting God who will establish, strengthen and perfect you?[9]

He will be to you what He says, but you need to know Him in a personal and intimate way. Because your life is hidden with Christ in God, that Christ-in-you is your hope of glory. He is the door to your salvation and the bread-of-life that satisfies your hungry soul. He is the Almighty God, the One who knows your beginning and ending. He is the only Supreme Ruler and your faithful witness. He is the Light of your world, the Presence of your serenity and the Peace of your life. He is the Lion from the tribe of Judah, the one who gives you the boldness to go forward in life without fear of intimidation from the adversary. He is the sovereign One over all that concerns you.

And So Much More...

He is the guardian of our pathway, and the forerunner who has gone ahead of us to level all crooked paths and order our steps so we are not overtaken by evil. He is our great High Priest, ushering us into the presence of the Most High God. He is the sacred servant who stooped so low that we might reign with Him in life and eternity. He is the representation of God, the Everlasting King who brings eternity to our lives. No matter what happens on this side of Heaven, in Him we have eternal life right here, right now on earth. He is the Lamb of God: the one who took away the sins of the world.

We have access to the presence of Father God because His eternal sacrifice has consecrated us, and made us flawless enough to stand before His holy place. He is our source, who feed us with productivity and substance. He is the truth, and when we come to Him, all lies cease to exist. He is the magnificent counselor, who shows us what quality decisions to make about life. When we have Him, we don't need all those "other counselors." He is the consolation of Israel: the one who wraps His hands around us when life hands us sour grapes that threaten to corrode the smile on our faces.

He is the Word of God that illuminates our path. He is the Arm of God, who executes justice on behalf of those whose hearts are perfect towards Him. He is the Apostle of our confession. When we come to Him, no weapon fashioned against us prospers. He is our Everlasting Father: many fathers have walked away from their homes and responsibilities, but this Father remains steadfast. He is the Ancient of Days, the one who was, is and is to come. He never shifts from His position of authority. He is the One who has guaranteed our passing over from the bondage of Egypt (death) into the Promised Land (life). When we come to Him, we find rest for our weary souls. He is so much more, but you need to find that out for yourself. When you seek Him, He promised that you would find Him.[10] Do you want to know Him or are you just content hearing about Him? When you come to knowledge of the One whom you are waiting upon, His life will become magnified through you and then your life becomes meaningful.

Invest Quality Time Seeking Him

When you do not have personal knowledge of the Lord, there is no way you are going to experience depth in your relationship with Him. If you don't seek Him, you will not be able to comprehend the level that will amazingly transform your life. There is so much that the Lord wants to show and tell you, but you must be in a love relationship with Him. Have you ever seen two people in love? They spend so much time sharing and caring for one another; the more time they spend together, the more they get to know one another. There is no exception to this rule: God can only reveal Himself when you spend intimate with Him in worship, prayer and service. Know that He rewards those who diligently seek him. There is a need for you to learn and keep learning truths about God.

God's people perish for lack of knowledge, therefore you must commit in your heart to not go through life without an intimate relationship with Him and the power of His resurrection. Tremendous gain and power comes with spending time in His presence. Begin to seek and yearn for Him, and you will be amazed at what happens in your life. When you dare to step out in faith and seek the Lord, He will come to you in all His glory and show His salvation. The original word for salvation is "soteria," which is an all-inclusive word that signifies forgiveness, healing, prosperity, deliverance, safety, rescue, liberation and restoration. Christ salvation is a total scope for the total man: spirit, soul and body.[11] When you come to God's saving knowledge, these are the benefits that you enjoy and much more. Therefore, I implore you to make His presence a primary pursuit in your life. When you set out to seek God, He will beautify the seasons and reasons of your life. You can toil all you want, but if you are not walking with God, all your efforts will overwhelm you and eventually be in vain. He is the answer to our yesterday, our today and tomorrow. Simply put, He is our all in all.

He is Your All in All

When you fix your gaze on God, He becomes your life's strength and anchor. Your arms will be made strong by the power of the Almighty God. Whatever you do in this life, let it be God who is continually strengthening and guiding you. Have you ever stopped to consider why your life has been so weak? God is full of power and anointing, and He wants you to walk in the divine capability that will make tremendous power available to your entire encounter with life. He wants you to experience His resurrection power, which brings life back to dead situations. He wants to resurrect issues in your life that other people have given up on.

I still vividly remember that, years ago, someone said to me, "Lami, you are worthless." Those words haunted me for a long time until I discovered what God had to say concerning me. When I discovered God's own version for the definition of my life, I have since become and done almost everything they said I would never do or become. He has deposited so much worth and value in my life, and I have not ceased to walk in the reality of His Word. Someone may have written you, but God resurrects issues by breathing life on them.

God wants to make manifest the exceeding greatness of His power towards those of us who believe.[12] When you see His power operating today, you will marvel at how awesome it is when He shows up again in your life. God's power is always greater than when you last encountered it. Your path is meant to shine brighter and brighter unto a perfect day, so to walk in integrity of God's word will move you from the pit to the palace. The power of which I speak is what released our Lord Jesus Christ from the clutches of death. When that power hit His body, death could not hold Him down. When you encounter the exceeding greatness of His power, you cannot be held back by death, decay, lack, confusion, brokenness and words of discouragement.

So awesome is this power that it quickened Abraham's dead loins and Sarah's worn out womb. Humanly speaking, child-bearing for them at an elderly age was an impossible mission. Yet, they did bear the promised child, Isaac, after 25 years of waiting on the promise. Your issues may not have human definitions, but the power of the living God will resurrect them: it's the power that causes the lame man to walk, the blind to see and dead to rise. When you let His presence become a primary pursuit in your life, He will become your all in all.

Do Weary Moments Show Up in the Midst of Your Search?

No matter our righteousness, we do become tempted to get weary amidst seeking Him, trusting Him and yearning for Him. Life is a constant battle of pain, grief, laughter and joy. When you see the multitudes coming against you, you may be tempted to believe that you have no power against them. As a matter of fact, you seem to be sinking, and you are, but only in your own powerless strength to challenge these multitudes. The flesh wants you to get weary and give up. At this point, you must come to that definite place in your relationship with Him of knowing that you are made to reign in life. You must make the commitment to wait on Him with a passion.

But Those Who Wait On The Lord

God will lead[13] and teach you to depend on Him in the midst of the chaos and turbulence of life. You learn to trust Him when you wait on Him because He sees what is ahead. You will receive strength[14] as you continue in His presence, but strength is not all you receive. As a matter of fact, everything pales in comparison to the deep revelations you will have of Him and the relationship you will cultivate by waiting on Him.

Growth and Development Unto All Things

As you wait on the Lord, you will mature in the things of God; as you continually spend time with Him, you will grow unto perfection. You will leave behind elementary principles of Christ: these fundamental doctrines are important to understand, but you need to go beyond elementary doctrines to make any significant spiritual progress.[15] When you can move beyond the basics, you will be able to reach higher. You will grow in grace and knowledge because the more time you spend with God, the more you will understand about His grace. You will add virtue to your faith and knowledge. You will grow through the Word of God: *"As new born babes, desire the pure milk of the Word that you may grow thereby."*[16] The growth factor in the waiting period is in the Word of God, and you cannot progress spiritually without Scripture. With the Word daily abiding and increasing in you, you will also grow in fruitfulness. God will increase and multiply you,[17]and this increase will come as you wait on Him and deposit the Word into your spirit.[18] Your life will have direction as you relate with Him, and You will grow and abound in love. What makes waiting on the Lord joyous and complete is the fact that those who diligently seek Him do find him. My heart's desire is that as you walk with Him, you will put away childish things and cultivate a deeper understanding of God, so you can find Him in every step of the way.

Spiritual Empowerment

Empowerment comes from the knowledge you have of Him, and time spent in intimate relationship with Him. Once you are full of power, you will triumph over physical forces that come against you, because God's unusual spiritual power works miracles by your hands.[19] You will be empowered with boldness to give witness of the Lord, due to the deposit of spiritual power you get from His presence.[20] This power will enable you speak and demonstrate the wisdom of God, because the Holy Spirit will accomplish what you were powerless to do. You will experience the riches of God's glory and be strengthened with might in your inner man. The Holy Spirit will empower you with soundness of mind.[21] Fear will become edged out of your life. God is going to strengthen you according to His word.[22] He has the armory for life's battles and He alone can subdue what comes against you, but you must trust Him. You will not need to fear anything, because He has promised to be there.[23] He will continue to search your heart and lead you in His everlasting ways.

He Becomes Your Source

People look to everything but God for satisfaction. This is very tragic because the preacher of Ecclesiastics made us realize that everything in life is vanity: that means everything is useless unless God is your source of existence. As you learn to consistently wait on the Lord, He becomes your source of power. If that power does not come from Him, you will fail because He gives us the power[24] to get wealth, "a state of being rich" in your spirit, soul, body and all that you lay your hands to do. In your season, you will bear rich fruits that enhance your life. If God is not the source of that power, you are headed for destruction. Nothing in creation has been designed to protect you, except the Lord your God. By waiting, you will make Him the source of your ability and strength. Refuse to change your position even when you cannot visibly see a way out. When you hold on, you will see the difference He will make in your life.

Another dimension of power comes with fasting that pleases God and praying in other tongues. See this power demonstrated in the story of the boy who had the mute spirit.[25] When the demonic spirit latched onto this boy, it caused him to go into a fit; the convulsing spirit left with great difficulties and bruised the young lad in the process. The boy's father was quite disheartened about what had befallen his child. So, he spoke to the disciples, but they could no do anything about this disturbing issue. They brought the boy to Jesus and the father told Him that his only wish was for the boy to be healed. Jesus then rebuked the demon out of the boy and the spirit obeyed, never to return. Jesus was not so impressed with His disciples because if had they built up their most holy faith, then casting out the demon would not have been an issue. The fasting and praying was not to cast out the demon, but to build up their faith.

When Jesus did all His work at Calvary, He won every battle you and I would ever have had to fight. You never have to spend a fraction-of-a-second praying and fasting to cast out any demon, for you already have dominion over them. You need to fast and pray to be able to do only what faith can do when threatened with unbelief. The disciples had a problem with unbelief, but prayer and fasting was that antidote. For more on the disciples' fast, refer to *Fasting for Spiritual Breakthrough* by Elmer Towns.[26] When situations are not giving way to your desired peace, remember that some situations cannot take a different turn except through prayer and fasting.

YOU FIND SPIRITUAL RENEWAL WAITING ON HIM

Keeping the right attitude is important as you wait on God. Much can go wrong if you engage in grumbling, complaining and murmuring, and testing God in your heart. The children of Israel[27] spent time complaining against the Lord. In spite of all He did for them in Egypt and all the miracles they saw, the Israelites were not patient enough to see where He was taking them. They spoke against Him, and refused to trust in His salvation. Eventually, they fell out of grace and kindled His anger against them. "When He slew them, then they sought Him; and they returned and sought earnestly for God." He wouldn't have slain any one of them, if only they had waited patiently. Sometimes, waiting on the Lord may be discouraging because you feel as if you are not moving forward. Then, you feel the temptation to complain against Him. But if you know that your later days will be better than those in the beginning, you will wait in patience and, as you do so, will experience spiritual renewal. You must learn to shut down voices of discouragement by the enabling of the Holy Ghost. When your spirit is silent and still before God, he renews you spiritually.

God has good plans for His children. He has pleasing plans that will give us an expected end. He wants us to be people with renewed, transformed, clear, holy and pure minds. We can only achieve this by offering ourselves to Him as living sacrifices[28] for His service. As we do this, we will have no desire to live by the world's standard. We will live daily by doing what God has called us to do and never conform to any mode of operation other than God's. So as not to get entangled in the world's system of operation, He gives grace to see us through every step of the way. You will get to the point where you live above the world's selfish, corrupt standards because of the anointing upon your life. The Holy Spirit will empower you to live by continually being transformed as you apply the wisdom of God's word to your heart. As you stay in the Word, your inward man is being renewed day-by-day. You will begin to think, walk, talk, behave in the way that God wants you to. Looking into the Word daily is to peer into the perfect law of liberty, and see what is able to build you up and give you an inheritance. The Word builds up cracks, broken dreams, and broken hearts, and does so simply by building you up.

Different Modes for Waiting on the Lord

Maintaining a Spiritual Warfare Position

To maintain a spiritual warfare position,[29] you ought to be found standing prepared for another battle after every attack thrown at you by the enemy. You wait on the Lord with a readiness to stand, and keep standing when all is said and done. We can see clearly that the battles we are up against are battles against invisible powers, which have a hierarchy of authority. At every level of growth in waiting on the Lord, you will be confronted with different levels of principalities, powers, rulers of the darkness, and against spiritual host of wickedness. Our Lord Jesus Christ has already won the battle against these powers that be. They have no dominion whatsoever over you, but you need to know that. You must take on the whole armor of God to be able to maintain a battle position. Refuse to be moved when you go over hurdles. Keep standing, and never let down your prayer guard. God expects us to watch and pray so we do not fall into the enemy's trap. Shut in alone with God in prayer so as to gain new levels of strength for new battles that will come against you. The war you are fighting in is the battle to still be "found standing" when the works of darkness challenges you.

Rest in His Presence

When you lie down in His presence, which is "a state of serene quietness,"[30] you will find rest for your soul. You are at rest, because you know that He is in control. You are not running around in a fretful state with no anchor of strength. Your rest will occur in choice green pastures, and your strong tower will leads you to still paths. As you learn to lie down in His presence, there will be no turbulence that you will not overcome. Most Christians are pretty much in a hurry. If you find yourself in this category, I encourage you to calm down, sit still at the Master's feet to hear His words.[31] In the story of Mary and Martha, one was busy about what the Master would eat, but the other was more concerned about sitting at the feet of Jesus to get His word into her spirit. Do you sit at the Master's feet daily? Is listening to His word of any significance to you? Begin to cultivate the right attitude towards His presence. Jesus is not here in person, but His Word is here with us, which is why you will need the Word of God to dwell richly within you.

Intimacy with Him

Because of the atoning blood of Lord Jesus Christ, we have access to His presence to commune and fellowship with Him.[32] Such fellowship is possible because He has cleansed us from all sin, during the very moment we confessed our sins to Him. As long as we walk in the light of who we are in Him now—that is, as new creatures—we can have fellowship with one another. The blood of Jesus is so precious. In the blood, we have found true cleansing and restoration that brings light in our lives. We discover the strength of intimacy with Him as we connect in fellowship with Him.

Letting Go of Weights

Progressively going up in our walk with God is a race of faith. In running this race, you need to lay aside every weight that has hindered you from getting to the place He has called you to.[33] You must do away with what has prevented your faithfulness from going forward. You alone know what I am talking about. Examine your life and ask God for grace to lay aside these weights so that you can run effectively. Think about what has kept you in bondage. I want to encourage you that you will not fail: just continue faithfully in this race, and hold on to the One who is able to keep you from falling.

This race is all about patience: lots of opportunities will present themselves for you to quit. But when you look at the big picture ahead, you will refuse to quit. Be determined in your heart to continually look up to the Lord Jesus. He is the Head of the heroes of faith. They are faithful witnesses because they looked up to God and overcame. He will be your head, perfecting every move you make. He has made you to be an overcomer: do not shift your gaze from Him. Observe and analyze every part of His life and the conduct you have seen in Scripture. Jesus was courageous in all even to the point of suffering. For the joy set before Him, He endured the cross, with all its suffering and shame. The will of the Father is to redeem creation, and this redemption caused Jesus to go to Calvary. Do you know the joy that is set before you? When you consider what Jesus did, you will know the joy set before you. This joy will enable you to do the Father's will, and put aside weights so that you do not falter.

Waiting On The Lord Mounts You Up for Exaltation

Even the youths shall faint and be weary, and the young men shall utterly fall, But those who wait on the Lord shall renew their strength; They shall mount up with wings like eagles, They shall run and not be weary, They shall walk and not faint.[34]

At some point in their lives, even the most vigorous, power-filled men will cave in and faint. But because you dared to wait on the Lord, you will not be overwhelmed to the point of hopelessness and desperation. God's promise is that your strength will be renewed. You will go high in life, and mount up with wings like the eagles. When you run in the race-of-faith, you will not get weary. You will walk through valleys, shadows, dark clouds, trials, temptations and pressures, but through them all will not faint. God will set you high above nations, and your name will be lifted up in praise and honor. If you only knew God's plans for you, you would hold onto Him and be patient.

All that you are going through now is a set up for your exaltation. God is going to exalt you beyond your wildest imaginations. God will exalt you so that people around you may know that He called you to show forth the many faces of His wisdom,[35] and that He is with you. God will exalt you relationally, emotionally, financially, physically, and materially. He is going to do things in your life that will cause people to wonder and say to themselves "Is this not the one we used to know?" When your exaltation comes, it will cause people to reverently fear the name of the Lord. They used to know you as the one who was so broke and well below average. You could hardly make ends meet. They knew you to be one who wore the same clothes day in and day out. You were known as the one whose life did not amount to anything. In looking at you, they know that ordinarily you should have lost your mind. You should have been eating out of garbage cans, and, eventually, locked up in an asylum. You should have been going through a divorce, or hung up on drugs like a junkie who could not remember his own name. They knew you so well: your children were acting like they have no sense at all, and your husband was sleeping around with anything in a skirt. You should have simply given up on life.

But how mighty and awesome God is. He singled you out, took away your shame and gave you a name. As you continue to walk with God, He will completely turn around things in your life for His glory. He will raise you from the dust for the purpose of setting you among princes. You will go to places you never thought possible. God is the Creator of the heavens and the earth: He will fix thrones here on earth for you. Your end will be better than your beginning. God will cause your name to be great and your fame will spread out. You will become increasingly prominent for the sake of the Gospel. God will increase your greatness and comfort on every side. He will deliver you and set you on high because you know His name. You will be lifted from your needs: they will not overwhelm you or pull you down. The Lord's blessings upon you will pass from generation to generation. Your supply shall never run dry. In you are rivers of living water, which will flow freely and never cease. Promotion will come to you. You will shine forth like the star, because the Lord will be your strength and He will give you authority over much.

ENDNOTES

1. Genesis 1:1
2. Exodus 34:5-6
3. Psalm 23:1
4. Ezekiel 48:35
5. Judges 6:24
6. Genesis 22:14

7. Exodus 17:15-16
8. Exodus 31:13
9. 1 Peter 5:10
10. Psalm 63:1-5
11. Extract from the Spirit Filled Bible; NKJV, p.1682, Thomas Nelson, Inc.
12. Ephesians 1:19
13. Psalm 25:5
14. Psalm 27:14
15. Hebrew 6:1, 2
16. 1 Peter 2:2
17. 2 Corinthians 9:8
18. Colossians 1:10
19. Zechariah 4:6; Acts 19:11,12
20. Acts 4:33
21. 2 Timothy 1:7
22. Psalm 119:28
23. Isaiah 41:10
24. Nelson's New Illustrated Bible Dictionary, p. 1021, (Thomas Nelson's Publishers Nashville)
25. Luke 9:37-42
26. Fasting for Spiritual Breakthrough, by Elmer L. Towns; (p. 31-33) Regal Books, a division of Gospel Light, Ventura, California, U.S.A. Printed in the U.S.A)
27. Psalm 78:1-35
28. Romans 12:1,2
29. Ephesians 6:10-14
30. Psalm 23:2
31. Luke 10:38-42

32. 1 John 1:7
33. Hebrew 12:1
34. Isaiah 40:30-31
35. 1 Peter 2:9

Soul Search

1. Have you cultivated a personal and intimate relationship with the One you are waiting on?

2. What promises of His are you enamored by?

3. What is the quality of time you invest in seeking His face and not His hands?

4. Have you been growing in the Word lately?

5. When did you last experience a spiritual renewal in His presence?

6. When faced with pressures, are you resting, fellowshipping, maintaining a battle stance in His presence?

7. What do you think is responsible for your lack of exaltation from on High?

CHAPTER 8

God Is Waiting To Give Us Good Things in His Presence

Always remember that God is good, no matter what has happened to you. The facts of your situation will never change who God is, because He is constant and unlimited, even in portions of your life that have been stressed out. You can always ask God for spiritual, emotional, material and physical strength. Whatever it is, ask God to meet you at the point of that need. The Father will withhold no good thing from those who walk uprightly. When it seems as if His response is delayed, it is to give us time to create a deeper insight into what we think we need; sometimes, what we think we need may not be good for us after all. Time spent in His presence will enlarge our appreciation for His answer, and finally allow us time to mature into what God wants us so we can use His gifts to bring beauty and exaltation to His name.

When you have knowledge of God's goodness within, you will never get to the point of trading your waiting period for the pleasure of any sin. Always take consequences of your actions into consideration before you do anything: if you trade the lasting benefit of the joy of God's presence for immediate gratification, the long-range consequence may not sit too well with you. We face all kinds of pressure daily, but should a momentary pressure distort the hope of your calling? Right now, the greatest need in your life is to find a focal point, which is God. Your relationship with Him will give you a purpose for daily living. When you establish relationship with Him, it will be easy to experience His goodness because He does not withhold anything from those who walk uprightly. King David walked with God to the point where he understood that His goodness[1] is forgiveness, healing, ransom, satisfaction, providence and much more.

God's goodness of is so deep that He desires for us to walk daily in a state of forgiveness, completely washed and redeemed by the blood of the Lamb. He wants us to walk in divine health because he has redeemed us from eternal destruction. There is so much heartache and pain upon the face of this earth, but God's goodness does not wish that on any one of His children. You can only truly live in divine health if you bask in His presence daily. I have always said that God comes to us with power when we allow Him step into our lives. As long as you dwell in His presence, no harm can come near your dwelling place.[2]

God also has satisfaction for our soul in store for us. His presence is satisfying, I tell you. If we stay in His presence, we will never walk in discontentment. What we do, and the people we are in relationship with are not supposed to burden to us; they are to become a part of fulfilling God's abundant life for us. Because we have God's nature residing on the inside, He really wants us to have a fulfilled life here on earth.[3] The Good Lord does not shortchange anyone who waits on Him. *Though your answers may tarry, they will surely come*. When you forsake all and come to Him, He will give you back a 100-fold what you left behind for righteousness sake. He is calling on you today to come to Him, and that reward is with Him.

As you Hear his voice beckoning you to come into His presence, do not harden your heart. He loves you enough, and He is waiting with open-wide arms for you to take the bold step into His presence. If you draw near to Him, He will draw near to you. It doesn't matter where you are in your life right now, or what you have done, are doing and planned to do, God knows everything. He knows about your pains, and He cares enough to have sent His only begotten son Jesus Christ. Having died on the Cross for your trespasses, He desires to make you whole in spirit, soul and body. My heart's cry is that you will hand everything over to God and watch Him turn your world around into the wholeness that eternity designed for you.

If you have read *Wait on the Lord* and do not have a personal relationship with Jesus Christ and don't even know where to begin, I want you to pray this prayer by faith. As you pray, He will come into your heart and make you a new person. He will do so by recreating your nature. He steps in with His nature, which is true, pure, holy and just.

> *Therefore, if anyone is in Christ, he is a new creation; old things have passed away; behold, all things have become you.*[4]

PRAYER

Dear Heavenly Father, I realize that I cannot even begin to wait on you because I do not have personal relationship with you. Therefore, today, I ask you, dear Jesus Christ, to come into my heart and make me a new person like you promised you would. I believe that You died, were buried and resurrected that I might have life in You. I also believe that you are Christ, the Son of the

Living God. I ask that you forgive me of my sins, wash me and make me clean. Fill me with the Holy Spirit, create in me a clean heart and renew the right spirit within me. Thank You for coming into my heart. I surrender my all to You and I hand over Lordship of my life to you. In Jesus name, I pray. Amen!

Congratulations, you are now born of God's Spirit and into his family.

ENDNOTES

1. Psalm 103:1-19
2. Psalm 91:9-10
3. John10: 10
4. 2 Corinthians 5:17

Epilogue

When the title of this book was first impressed on my Spirit in prayer, I did not fully comprehend its use. Many books have been written and many messages preached about waiting on the Lord. But God showed me that this was not just to be "another" book about waiting on Him. Instead, it is a message of His divine presence and the desire for His children to walk and live in that presence. Several times, I tried in my own ability to change the book's title and, at such times, I can't describe to you the shallow feelings I experienced in my guts. I settled upon the issue of God's original title and went to work.

As days turned to weeks and weeks turned to months, I found myself typing away as the very things I wrote about were being challenged by "contrary evidences." I had two options: to hold on to what I strongly believed in my spirit, or to let the devil lie on the book.

One Sunday afternoon, I had this verses burnt into my spirit and I quickly wrote it down: *"He told them not to depart from Jerusalem, but to wait* (stay around; await)[1] *for the promise of the father, 'which' He said, you have had from me."*[2] He said to me that waiting comes with my promise and it's my divine assurance. Right there and then, I knew that what you profess with your mouth will be challenged. But you are to wait amidst visible signs of contrary evidences and get to the Father's promise.

As you step out in faith to wait on the Lord, the last thought I would like to leave you with is this: do not waver away from His presence. Keep your mind determined and consistently focused to wait on Him at all times, and never go back to leaning on your own understanding, even if life's complexities pose barriers on your path. Be constant with the Lord amidst storms because *storms don't last forever*. After every storm comes calm, therefore be prepared to trust in the One who is able to keep you from falling and can present you complete before the everlasting throne of glory.

ENDNOTES

1. Greek Dictionary of the New Testament, PG 57. [The Hebrew-Greek key Word study Bible, King James Version. AMG Publishers Chattanooga, TN 37422, USA]
2. Acts 1:4

Contact the Author

PLOT 2B, RAFIU BABATUNDE TINUBU ROAD,
OFF ADMIRALTY WAY LEKKI PHASE 1,
LAGOS NIGERIA

fralam25@hotmail.com

FAX:+234 1 270 8565

Books to help you grow strong in Jesus

JOHNNY ROCKET AND HIS COMRADES IN THE FAITH

By Matthew Botsford

Join a young boy's imaginative adventures in his intergalactic spaceship, The Regatta, with his "comrades in the faith," as they discover new worlds and civilizations while seeking to "save the world" as only a boy can imagine. Danger, sabotage, miracles, healings, and manifestations follow Johnny Rocket in his journeys, all the while revealing exciting, Biblically based moral realities. ISBN: 88-89127-07-4

WHAT DO YOU LEARN IN SCHOOL?

By Brian Watts

While public schools ingrain students with a secular worldview, Christian education should teach our children to think from a biblical worldview. This calls for a radical change in the way we approach curriculum. We must stop drawing from the world's curriculum and make the Bible our true foundation. Brian Watts provides insightful guidance regarding how to create a truly biblical curriculum so that our children will be equipped for a life of service and be able to view the world through the lens of God's Word. ISBN:88-89127-05-8

MY LEGACY

By Rowan McRae

My Legacy is an interactive journal that asks simple but provocative questions and will inspire you to remember important events, circumstances, and feelings in your own life. It also provides an incentive to evaluate your time used thus far and how to make better use of the time you have left. ISBN:88-89127-06-6

Order Now from Destiny Image Europe

Telephone: +39 085 4716623- Fax +39 085 4716622

E-mail: ordini@eurodestinyimage.com

Internet: www.eurodestinyimage.com

OVERCOMING TEMPTATION

By Manickam Chandrakumar

God has given us the power and the desire to resist the work of the enemy. Sin does not have to be a normal way of life. You can learn how to resist the temptation that leads to sin. The author has helped people in over sixty countries with the principles in this book.You can turn your defeat into victory, no matter how strong the temptation to sin might be in your life. This book will give you the keys to begin a life of true victory! ISBN:88-89127-03-1

WHERE ARE THE SONS IN THE HOUSE?

By Jerome Nel

Within the church, the concept of mentoring has existed throughout the ages. Spiritual fathers mentor their sons-both men and women-who then become fathers to the next generation. *Where are the Sons in the House?* examines the vital relationship of mentors (spiritual fathers) and mentees (spiritual sons and daughters) in the house of God. This book will allow you to clearly see your role in the local church and will inspire and challenge you to meet your full potential as a member of the body of Christ. This book will open your eyes to the truth of how satan so often manipulates the body of Christ and hinders her growth. If you are serious about becoming who God intends you to be, you must read this book! ISBN:88-89127-01-5

THE HOLE IN THE HEDGE

By Mario Marchiò

"*The Hole in the Hedge*" will help the reader understand the vital truth found in Scripture which states, "He who breaks a hedge, a snake will bite him!" The author brings clarity and solace where there was confusion and doubt while bringing you one step closer to the reality of the Gospel of Jesus Christ, which is, "God is good and He loves me." ISBN:88-89127-00-7

IN MY FATHER'S HOUSE

By Amanda Wells

Too many men of God today are deceived into a building a pedestal, whereby, they have to keep other men from either dethroning them or climbing on board with them. This is not about pride and arrogance. Let it never become about numbers, who has more, but let this apostolic move be about lives and the shaping of men and women into their God-given call and destinies, who leave an inheritance and legacy for our sons and daughters to walk in. ISBN: 88-900588-6-2

TRANSFORMATION AND DOMINION

By Lee LaCoss

Jesus says, "...upon this rock, I will build My church..." In this book we discover many ways that Jesus accomplishes this purpose in and through His people. We are confronted with real questions and issues, and are given practical, biblical answers and direction.

The Lord's "new creation humanity" is called to know Him, and to mature by expressing His nature and abilities as true overcomes in this life.

ISBN: 88-900588-7-0

FRIENDS, A GIFT FROM GOD
How to Maintain Healthy Relationships

By Ade Adesina

Relationships are fundamental in the race of life; they can easily be the making or conversely the breaking of any man. All seem to agree that, "no man is an island", however the solution is also often the problem, for the mismanagement of these relationships can negatively impact one's destiny. Many are living frustrated lives because of mismanaged relationships. Pastor Adesina in this insightful study, expatiates on the nature, purpose and modes of operation of the different types of relationships, and with practical steps, he places in one's hands the tools necessary to enjoy a healthy relationship with all. It is possible...discover now. ISBN: 88-900588-8-9

Order Now from Destiny Image Europe

Telephone: +39 085 4716623- Fax +39 085 4716622

E-mail: ordini@eurodestinyimage.com

Internet: www.eurodestinyimage.com